THE ONE THAT GOT AWAY

and Other LifeLessons from Fishing

Dan Bolin

NAVPRESS⬤
BRINGING TRUTH TO LIFE
NavPress Publishing Group
P.O. Box 35001, Colorado Springs, Colorado 80935

The Navigators is an international Christian organization. Our mission is to reach, disciple, and equip people to know Christ and to make Him known through successive generations. We envision multitudes of diverse people in the United States and every other nation who have a passionate love for Christ, live a lifestyle of sharing Christ's love, and multiply spiritual laborers among those without Christ.

NavPress is the publishing ministry of The Navigators. NavPress publications help believers learn biblical truth and apply what they learn to their lives and ministries. Our mission is to stimulate spiritual formation among our readers.

ISBN 1-57683-074-8

Cover illustration by Stanley Woodward/Wood River Media, Inc., San Rafael, CA

Some of the anecdotal illustrations in this book are true to life and are included with the permission of the persons involved. All other illustrations are composites of real situations, and any resemblance to people living or dead is coincidental.

Unless otherwise identified, all Scripture quotations in this publication are taken from the *HOLY BIBLE: NEW INTERNATIONAL VERSION* ® (NIV®). Copyright © 1973, 1978, 1984 by International Bible Society. Used by permission of Zondervan Publishing House. All rights reserved. Other versions used include: the *New American Standard Bible* (NASB), © The Lockman Foundation 1960, 1962, 1963, 1968, 1971, 1972, 1973, 1975, 1977; and the *King James Version* (KJV).

Printed in the United States of America

1 2 3 4 5 6 7 8 9 10 11 12 13 14 15 / 05 04 03 02 01 00 99 98

To my dad, Warren Bolin, who took me fishing.
To my mom, Jean Bolin, who cleaned my fish.
To my wife, Cay Bolin, who sits in the boat with me.
To my daughter, Haley Bolin, who has the patience to fish with me.

All four are wonderful examples of the Christian life.

Contents

PREFACE

Most men I know view time as a valuable commodity. The days fly by, spurred on by the pressures of work, family, church, and community service. Constant withdrawals from our bank accounts of time, energy, creativity, money, and talents can leave us spiritually bankrupt, with nothing more to give.

But there's a better way to live! It's possible to keep making deposits to our accounts and avoid bankrupting our spiritual lives.

Unfortunately, we've got to do it "on the fly."

The Air Force understands this dilemma. When planes must travel long distances, they can't carry enough fuel to reach their destinations. With normal refueling impossible, pilots have learned to refuel in flight. A temporary solution for unusual circumstances, but it works.

This book is about refueling in flight. It offers short devotional thoughts to refuel your spiritual life while you're on the fly. The entries are short enough to be read between appointments, as people line up outside your door, as you rush through a quick lunch. They're good before and after any pressure points in your daily schedule.

I've certainly had fun writing these pages. Thinking back over the years of fishing has been a delight as I've replayed the memories of good times with family and friends. I've recalled getting out of bed while every other human with normal faculties is still sleeping comfortably. I've stood for hours in ice-cold water, slapped at a million mosquitoes, acquired countless sunburns, and consumed far too many soggy sandwiches. I've even driven for hours, only to realize I'd left the tackle box at home. Thinking back, I'm not sure why the memories are so wonderful, but they are. I hope you will experience just as much pleasure in the reading as I've had in the writing. Many of the events in the book are autobiographical. I have taken the liberty to remember the stories to my advantage.

Finally, I offer a few heartfelt thank yous. Steve Webb with NavPress has been a great encouragement. Dana Bertino read, typed, reread, retyped, and was a great source of insight — and she can spell. Sue Geiman and Gary Wilde added their genius. I'll take any blame, give them any credit.

My wife, Cay, and daughter, Haley, encouraged and critiqued my thoughts as the book progressed. They also let me use our home computer while their projects and games waited.

It would also be unfair if I did not mention the hundreds of speakers who have been a part of Pine Cove Christian Camps over the years. I have been privileged to hear outstanding teachers for the past twenty-five years. Their messages and the notes scrawled in the margins of my Bible have been a source of insight and have provoked many of the thoughts I have shared in this book. I'm not a great original thinker, but I have been able to forget which speaker said what.

DAN BOLIN
August 1997

Introduction

When I was five years old I caught my first fish. In fact, that day I caught lots of fish. My pole had no reel, only a short length of heavy cloth fishing line tied to the top eyelet with a weight and hook attached. I caught fish, and fishing caught me. From day one I was hooked.

That same year I understood enough about spiritual things to know that if I died I would not go to heaven. In a simple, unsophisticated manner, under the covers in my bed, I asked Jesus to come into my heart. I'd say things differently today, but back then I didn't have the advantage of Bible school, Christian college, and seminary. It was an appropriate start for a five-year-old boy who didn't want to go to hell.

So began two pilgrimages—the life of a Christian and the life of a fisherman. Neither started with much ceremony or dignity, but both life choices gave direction to my life.

Throughout my developmental years I remember setting my heart on fishing. There was nothing I looked forward to more than the next time I could put a hook in the water. This of course excluded Christmas and birthdays. At Christmas my stocking was filled with hooks and sinkers; and my summer birthdays were celebrated camping at Frog Lake or some other trout-infested body of water.

Setting one's heart on fishing means being absorbed with the next chance to fish. It means drawing pictures of fish on the bulletins during church services and talking to anyone who will listen about the one that got away.

Fishing was more than a heart exercise. Becoming a skilled fisherman required setting my mind on fishing as well. I organized and reorganized the tackle box, sharpened the knife, kept a card catalogue of the places I'd fished, made notes about what lures had worked and what I had learned about each lake and stream. I wanted to know everything I could about fish — especially how to catch them.

It was never difficult to keep my mind focused on fishing. In the fourth grade I had the world's worst teacher. This woman had a special gift. She was one of maybe only a handful of teachers in the world who could make Oregon State history boring to a nine-year-old boy. Joe Meek, Lewis and Clark, explorers, fur traders, and wagon trains were reduced to an outline to be copied from the chalkboard. We were even graded on our penmanship. Somehow I survived social studies but I wasn't quite so lucky with math. At the end of the year I couldn't convince my mother that a "D" was the best possible grade under the circumstances. Mom sentenced me to math workbooks one hour a day all summer long. She could make me do math with my pencil but in my head I was fishing.

My heart and mind were set on fishing from an early age. This foundation was the basis for many of my life decisions.

The other half of my pilgrimage has been much more bumpy. I wish I could say that my heart and mind have been set on loving and knowing Christ since childhood. There have been times when Christ has been important to me, and there have been times when my heart has been stone cold toward Him and my mind has wandered elsewhere. I have long stretches of history when I pushed the pause button on my spiritual life (only to find that there is no pause button — only forward or reverse).

Moving forward with my Christian life has required more intentionality than my fishing life. Fishing became my undisciplined response to unstructured time and opportunity. Cultivation of my spiritual life has required a great deal more structure and discipline.

This cultivation creates significant tension in any believer's life. How do we discipline ourselves to love and know God without losing the vitality and reality that we desire from our relationship with God? How do we go through the motions of spending time with God without falling into a mindless and heartless rut? There are two parts to one answer. The first part is that without some structure and discipline we will not achieve what we want from our walk with God. However, the second part of the answer balances the first; if our relationship with God is merely a brief thought tossed toward heaven in the morning or evening and God is walled off from the rest of our lives, then we have settled for ritual and missed the reality. The answer is that Christ wants our focus. He wants us to lock our attention on Him the way I locked my heart and mind on fishing. Not once a day but all day, not one day a week but every day of our lives.

Focusing on fishing has always been easy for me, but I need help focusing and refocusing on Christ. Loving and knowing Christ is infinitely more important than loving and knowing fishing. I need help to keep myself focused on Christ, all day every day, because where I set my heart and mind influences everything in my life.

Since, then, you have been raised with Christ, set your hearts on things above, where Christ is seated at the right hand of God. Set your mind on things above, not on earthly things. For you died and your life is now hidden with Christ in God. (Colossians 3:1-3)

The apostle Paul's command is not optional. We have been given a directive to set our hearts and minds on Christ and the things pertaining to His world. I hope this book will help you set your heart and mind on the things of God. I assume that those who read this are similar like me. My guess is that you have hearts and minds already set on fishing but wish they were more focused on Christ. For thirty-one days you can think about fishing and think about God. Thinking about Christ when you think about fishing may never become automatic, but I hope in some small way this book helps redirect your thoughts to the Carpenter who taught others to be fishers of men.

Note to the Reader: You can use this book in a variety of ways. Of course, you might choose to read a chapter a day for a month. Great! But don't limit yourself to that kind of rigorous reading plan if your schedule would tend to make it a chore.

In that case, try these options:

- Read a chapter a week for thirty-one weeks, perhaps on a Saturday night before Sunday worship.

- Read chapters with a group of friends and discuss your reactions and insights together—whenever you can meet.

- Read every time you go fishing, or whenever you think about fishing.

- Or . . . just read when the Spirit moves you

Reading this book ought to be like taking a breath of fresh air whenever you need it. So no matter how you plan your devotional times, let them become quality visits with the Lord.

ONE

LIFE IN THE TACKLE BOX

MY FATHER'S TACKLE BOX ALWAYS FASCINATED ME. IT WAS A big, green, plastic case with a brass latch and two trays that automatically folded out when you opened the lid. It overflowed with tackle and had an "organization" known only to us family members. This monstrosity housed a wide assortment of lures and equipment, and I wanted to open it and rummage through it every chance I got. Each piece of equipment had its own intrigue, and each lure represented a different adventure. Hooks, bobbers, sinkers, pocket knives, pliers, flies, leader, big shiny lures, and little spinners: each unique, each important.

I remember the birthday when I got my own tackle box. It was red, and much smaller than my dad's, but the latch came with a fantastic guarantee: good for a million openings! By the end of the day, Mom told me I'd already used up most of them.

My box had only one tray, and it didn't slide back automatically when opened. But like Dad's, it was filled with an assortment of hooks and sinkers along with odds and ends I'd retrieved from overhanging branches or submerged logs. The items' origins didn't concern me. I was only interested in whether or not I had enough of the right equipment to catch the fish I was after.

We Are Called to Cooperate . . .

We fishermen need our tackle boxes because several pieces of equipment must work together to fool a fish, and different fish require different lures. Each piece is valuable, designed for a specific purpose. Lures, leader, swivels, bobbers, hooks—each play a role the others can't perform. And each must cooperate with others to fulfill their designed function and contribute to a successful fishing trip.

Sometimes I think of all the unique individuals in the church, each designed by the Creator to perform a special task. And I realize that the Christian community is much like a tackle box. I imagine some folks as the shiny store-bought variety of lure, with lots of feathers and parts that twist and turn—complicated individuals. Others are picked out of a limb along the bank and are well weathered.

Of course, the metaphors for this interacting community of God's people are endless. The apostle Peter, for instance, pictures the church as bricks being built up to form a holy temple, with Christ as the cornerstone:

> *You also, like living stones, are being built up into a spiritual house to be a holy priesthood, offering spiritual sacrifices acceptable to God through Jesus Christ. For in Scripture it says, "See, I lay a stone in Zion, a chosen and precious cornerstone, and the one who trusts in him will never be put to shame." (1 Peter 2:5-6)*

And the apostle Paul uses the human body to illustrate complementary, unique parts working together to accomplish their designed potential:

If the whole body were an eye where would the sense of hearing be? If the whole body were an ear, where would the sense of smell be? But in fact God has arranged the parts in the body, every one of them, just as he wanted them to be. If they were all one part, where would the body be? As it is, there are many parts, but one body. (1 Corinthians 12:17-20)

But I love the tackle-box imagery. A combination of hooks, line, weights, and other equipment must cooperate and work together, contributing their functions to accomplishing the goal of catching a fish. Some lures are ideal for a particular fish in a certain situation. When circumstances change, the fisherman lays one lure aside and picks up another. This doesn't reflect poorly on the first lure, but it does say that the situation has changed. Other abilities are more appropriate for the need of the moment.

Similarly, each of us in God's tackle box has a gift to contribute to the church's prime goals: evangelism and mutual edification. We must apply ourselves to becoming the best we can be as we use the gifts we've been given, all the while appreciating the gifts of those around us, encouraging them to keep growing into the likeness of Jesus.

. . . But Are You Compelled to Compare?
It's good to dwell together in the body of Christ. But living as part of this great "tackle box," we do face an insidious threat. It is our compulsion to compare ourselves with the other "equipment" in the box. Comparison leads us to one of two destruc-

tive pitfalls: pride or pity. Either we become enamored with what God has given us and think too highly of ourselves, or we begin to envy what he has entrusted to someone else. We puff up with pride or pout with pity.

Instead of comparing my gifts with those of others, I'd like to spend more time in two productive endeavors. Will you consider joining me? First we can find ways to use our gifts to help others. God gave us those special abilities, not to mount them in our trophy case, but to benefit our fellow citizens in the kingdom.

Second, we can make a concerted effort to discover the gifts of those we interact with every day. What are the special gifts of the person who will sit in the pew next to you this Sunday morning? Who has exercised his or her gifts by serving the church well in the past few months? In other words, how well do you know your brothers and sisters in Christ?

There can be no Lone Ranger Christians because we need one another so much. Each of our gifts has its place. And we can make room for all of them to do their life-giving work.

FISHING DEEPER
READ ROMANS 12:3-8

- Why do you think Paul put the exhortation in verse three at the beginning of this section?
- What are your gifts, and how are you using them?

T W O

LEO THE LEATHER LIP

I LOVE WATCHING A CHILD CATCH HIS FIRST FISH. IT'S DELIGHTFUL!

Family campers at Pine Cove Christian Conference Center gather to fish and talk on a dock that reaches into a small private lake. The seat railing around the dock makes a great place for children to dangle their feet over the water while their fathers help them tempt sunfish with pieces of leftover breakfast sausage threaded on #8 hooks.

The red and white bobbers disappear time and again, but the fish steal the bait before the children can react. Sometimes, however, fish and child get together. As junior pulls his five-inch trophy onto the dock, kids squeal, mom cheers, and dad removes the hook. The fish is then released to delight another child while dining on a second helping of sausage.

This has happened so often that the camp staff members claim there's only one fish in the lake—Leo the Leather Lip. Leo is said to be well trained, allowing children to catch him in exchange for a never ending supply of leftover sausage.

Dangerous Patterns

I've known too many people like Leo. They seem to be happy doing the same dangerous things time and again.

Actually, I have a little bit of Leo in myself. No doubt each

21

of us does. Like Leo, any of us can grow to love the taste of sausage too much and be drawn back to the thing we said we would never do again. For some of us it's raging anger. For others it could be lust, pride, drugs, alcohol, possessions, even another person. Anything that is "saving" our lives for the moment can gain the upper hand and draw us away from the One who saves us for eternity. Then we make the same mistakes time and time again. The great apostle Paul understood this predicament. We don't know the particular sin he fought on a daily basis but, we can identify with his struggle. In Romans 6:11-14 he writes:

> *Count yourselves dead to sin but alive to God in Christ Jesus. Therefore do not let sin reign in your mortal bodies so that you obey its evil desire. Do not offer the parts of your body to sin . . . but rather offer yourselves to God. . . . For sin shall not be your master, because you are not under the law, but under grace.*

Paul knew that sheer willpower wouldn't work. He couldn't overcome the sin in his life without three things that go beyond a mere human ability to resist. First, he focused on the giver and sustainer of life, the one who makes us "alive to God in Christ Jesus." Sinful gratifications won't fulfill us because they make us feel alive only for the moment. Rather, the God of the universe, whom we know through His son Jesus Christ, gives us total and eternal life. True life comes only from God Himself, and no substitute satisfies as He does.

Second, Paul declared what God requires of us: "Offer yourselves to God." We must give ourselves to God if we are to be good stewards of what He has given us. When we contemplate the wonder of His character, we can do little more than offer Him all that we are.

Third, Paul stressed what God has done for us: "You are not under the law, but under grace." God's grace didn't quit working when He saved us. His grace is available to us as we need it. Grace supplies us with the power to live for Him in the face of the temptations that challenge us on a daily basis.

Delicious Alternative

Leo the Leather Lip became comfortable with a pattern of life that captured him over and over. He couldn't resist picking at what he thought would bring him satisfaction—the very thing that would kill him.

Yet by God's grace we can break the power of sin in our lives. When we encounter a tempting morsel, we can look for the hook. And we can remember the full satisfaction that comes from a relationship with God in Christ Jesus, all wrapped in the grace He gives to serve and obey Him.

Yes, His grace provides the relationship with God that satisfies the deepest desires of our hearts. When we're filled with all of His large and lavish good gifts, we lose our appetite for tiny dried-up crumbs of leftover sausage.

FISHING DEEPER
READ 1 CORINTHIANS 10:10-13

- What temptation are you facing these days?
- How willing are you to look for a way out?

THREE

EYES TO SEE

MY GRANDPA DROVE A 1954 PONTIAC CHIEFTAIN, AND IT WAS a tank.

Picture a dark-green-over-light-green sedan with a big bench seat in front. Straps hung just behind the rear doors and a cord ran across the back of the front seat for passengers to clench during the sharp curves. The car was loaded, a straight eight automatic; it even had a radio. Grandpa told me he paid $2,000 cash for the car. Not cash as in a check, but cash as in twenty-dollar bills.

Grandpa loved his grandchildren, loved to fish, and especially loved to fish with his grandchildren. When we couldn't go fishing he would drive us in the Pontiac to Foster's Sporting Goods on Lombard Street. Over the door hung a huge sign with a rainbow trout you could see from blocks away. We'd browse up and down the long aisles, and he would explain the use and purpose of the items on display. Then he'd buy us hooks and sinkers, bobbers and, lures. Nothing very expensive, but he kept us supplied with the basics.

Toward the end of his life, Grandpa's eyes began to fail him. I remember stopping by his house one day after school, as was my custom. After a half hour of the *Three Stooges* on TV, our conversation turned to fishing and to Foster's Sporting

Goods. Soon we were backing out of the driveway in the green tank. As we approached the light at Lombard Street, however, I knew something was wrong. "Is the light green or red?" Grandpa asked. "You tell me when it turns yellow."

There were only four or five lights between his house and Foster's, but each one was an adventure. As a pre-driver I had never gauged when a light would turn from green to yellow. Never considered how long it would *stay* yellow, either!

But I learned.

The trip home was equally exciting, but we came to no harm. Except that I blurted out the whole grand adventure to my family at the dinner table that evening.

And that was the last time Grandpa drove his '54 Pontiac Chieftain.

Tough Decision!

They say grandparents and grandchildren get along so well because they share a common enemy: the middle generation. My parents were forced to make a difficult choice that day. They had to take Grandpa's keys before he hurt himself or someone else. The real problem was his eyesight. He had eyes, but he couldn't see clearly enough to recognize potential dangers.

Have you noticed that the spiritual world and the physical world sometimes move in opposite directions? Our physical eyesight grows dim the longer we live but our spiritual vision improves as we walk with Christ day by day. Consider the events in Mark, chapter eight, for instance. Jesus confronted his disciples—after He had just fed thousands—when they complained that no one had brought bread for the boat ride across the Sea of Galilee. Here's His stern rebuke:

> *"Why are you talking about having no bread? Do you still not see or understand? Are your hearts hardened? Do you have eyes but fail to see?"* (verses 17-18)

The next event in the chapter (verses 22-25) is a very unique healing of a blind man. Jesus takes the man outside the city, isolating Himself with the man and His disciples. The healing is unusual because it takes place in two steps. No doubt Christ could have healed with one thought, one touch, or one word. But He had a purpose for demonstrating His power in two stages: to teach His disciples an important lesson. Through the first step the man moved from total darkness to a recognition of light. The second step provided perfect vision, and the details of life came into full view.

Two Steps for Him . . . and Us

Leaving the scene of the miracle, Jesus and the disciples hiked north. On the way, Jesus asked them, "Who do people say I am?" (Mark 8:27).

"You are the Christ," says Peter.

With this crucial truth established in their minds, Jesus began teaching them that He would suffer many things and eventually be killed. At that news, Peter's vision, once crystal clear, quickly turned blurry. In verse 32 we read, "Peter took him aside and began to rebuke him." This impetuous disciple understood Christ's identity but failed to comprehend the implications for every area of his life. In other words, Peter had moved from darkness to light but stopped short of the second step of spiritual development. Like the partially healed blind man, Peter was able to grasp some great truths, but he still needed 20/20 spiritual vision.

This can bring us to some sobering conclusions. It's obvious that moving from darkness to light can happen in a moment. But spiritual eyesight develops over a lifetime.

How do you rate your vision at the moment?

FISHING DEEPER
READ 2 CORINTHIANS 4:16-18

- What truth about God's character has grown clearer for you in recent years?
- How does this new perspective of God change your approach to a current problem you're facing?

FOUR

SILVER SALMON'S LAST LEAP

MY UNCLE CEEB COULD TELL STORIES ALMOST AS WELL AS he could fish. So, as a boy of twelve, I was never sure where the fish story ended and a fishy tale began.

One day while I was admiring his boat—a wonderfully seaworthy craft that had often challenged the surging coast-line swells of Siletz Bay to head into open sea—he began to tell me of a recent fishing excursion with a friend.

It seems the day was cold and the fishing fair. Silver salmon were jumping all around. Ceeb and his fishing buddy had hooked several but only one was in the boat. While trolling large flashers resembling herring, they kept in sync with other boats also working the dark, green water. The sound of the small trolling motors was punctuated by the slap of salmon exploding out of the water like submarine-launched missiles and falling back into the deep. Usually, this sound was the only evidence that salmon were in the area. But on this particular day, fish could be seen erupting around the boat, tantalizing the fishermen in every direction.

I was believing the story to this point, and then it got a little fishy.

"We were trolling along, minding our poles and our own business when a silver salmon came out of the water, jumped over the gunnel, and landed right in our laps"

I didn't know whether to go along with this preposterous story (and look foolish at the dinner table when Ceeb told the whole family how he had pulled one over on me) or whether to accuse my uncle of lying. After all, he was a deacon in the First Baptist church. I froze for a moment, then chose to go along.

I chose wisely. He had witnesses who supported his story. The fish had truly jumped into the boat (and from there into the frying pan!).

Great Expectations

The poor fish made one foolish mistake, and it was the last mistake he ever made.

Even though God is a God of second chances who specializes in showing His forgiveness and grace to those who need it, there are natural consequences to our actions. We see it all around us. AIDS or other sexually transmitted diseases, alcohol related traffic accidents, drug overdoses, and acts of violence. All are consequences of drastic behaviors.

Do we really believe in dire consequences anymore? Or have we become callused to the immorality, unethical business dealings, and debauchery on the part of our so-called heroes today? Unfortunately, we even see such behaviors in our Christian leaders. And, of course, the Scriptures are full of equally grievous scenarios:

- Adam and Eve ate of the forbidden fruit and were banished from the garden and given the sentence of death.

- Moses struck a rock with his staff instead of speaking to the rock and was not allowed to enter the Promised Land.
- Achan stole some silver and clothes and was stoned to death.
- King David murdered and committed adultery, thus bringing violence and calamity to his household.
- Gehazi lied and was given leprosy.
- Ananias and Sapphira deceived and dropped dead on the spot.

God has expectations for our behavior; He expects obedience.

It is so much better to avoid the mistakes of sin in the first place than to risk the irreparable damage that accompanies sheer willfulness. Yes, God generally provides second chances. But we never know when or if we are jumping in the wrong direction for the last time.

Strong to the End
Some mistakes are last mistakes. Yet instead of making final and fatal mistakes, we can realize that God wants us to finish strong. We can proceed in His strength.

Consider Caleb in this regard. He was a young slave in Egypt who distinguished himself to the point that he was selected to represent the tribe of Judah in scoping out the Promised Land. Ten spies brought back a negative prediction about a potential invasion. Only Caleb and Joshua trusted God to defeat their enemies and give them the land.

Ten spies made the mistake of doubting God's power and provision. Two trusted God and His promise of victory. The people listened to the majority report, and the Israelites were forced to wander in the desert for forty years until Caleb's generation had died out.

Caleb and Joshua were the only two of their generation allowed to enter the land and enjoy the benefits of God's provision. At eighty-five years of age Caleb remained faithful to God and went forward to accomplish all he could. He came to Joshua with his final request:

> So here I am today, eighty-five years old! I am still as strong today as the day Moses sent me out; I'm just as vigorous to go out to battle now as I was then. Now give me this hill country that the Lord promised me.
> (Joshua 14:10-12)

His request was granted; he finished strong.

Don't end your useful service to God by jumping in the wrong direction. Live the life of Caleb, strong to the end.

FISHING DEEPER
READ 2 KINGS 5:9-16, 19-27

- When have you committed a small act of rebellion or selfishness that created significant harm in your life?
- How willing are you to forego a self-centered interest in order to remain loyal to God's direction in your life?

FIVE

SMALL BUT SIGNIFICANT

THE BIGGEST TROUT I EVER CAUGHT WAS A TWENTY-TWO-INCH rainbow. He hit hard, took out most of my line, and turned and ran each time he saw my net. He was too majestic a warrior to eat or mount, so after taking a couple of pictures, I put him back in the water. He swam off with only a swollen lip and injured pride. On the other hand, my pride was swelling and my lips were flapping. I wanted to tell everyone about my trophy.

As I told the story, I realized the irony of catching a twenty-two-inch trout with a fly tied on a #22 hook. A hook that size is as small as they come. And the minuscule flies must be tiny to imitate the real bugs that provide breakfast, lunch, and dinner for trout.

I tried my hand at fly-tying years ago and soon discovered that those little hooks and my clumsy fingers were no match. I'll gladly pay an expert to tie my flies properly and avoid the time and aggravation. When it comes to these tiny hooks I'm "fly-tying challenged."

Without the tiny hook, though, I would never have caught my great big fish. Little tool, big job.

Consider Little Gideon
We shouldn't be shocked when pint-sized tools are used to

overcome giant challenges. Gideon was a little man, lowest on the social totem pole in Israel. In Judges chapter six he describes himself and his station in life like this: "My clan is the weakest in Manasseh, and I am the least in my family" (verse 15). Yet the Israelites faced a powerful enemy that had been making their lives miserable for years. The Midianites, Amalekites, and other nations from the East marched to Israel every year, attacking the cities and raiding the farms. And each year the Israelites were left starving. Their foe was again amassing a huge army to invade their land, grab their property, and threaten their lives.

Somebody needed to step up to the challenge.

Thus the Angel of the Lord approached Gideon as he hid in a remote wine press, protecting his meager harvest. "The Lord is with you, mighty warrior" (verse 12), announced the Angel.

Can't you just see the young farmer doing a classic, "Who . . . *me*?" What a wide-eyed double take that must have been! In the first place, Gideon didn't believe that God was with him. And second, what's all this "mighty warrior" talk? A life of pain and poverty had likely convinced Gideon that God was far away, if He existed at all. The terror that controlled the simple tasks of his life left him feeling small and weak. Gideon looked at his situation and responded with two logical questions, "If the Lord is with us, why has all this happened to us? Where are all his wonders that our fathers told us about?" (verse 13).

Of course, God demonstrated His power several times in an attempt at bolstering the young man's faith. When Gideon gathered 32,000 men, God said the army was too big and reduced it to 10,000. Not a great way to inspire confidence in this reluctant new leader. The odds had become worse for the outnumbered and ill-trained Israelite army, but again God said the force was too big. By the time the Lord finished, Gideon stood before an army of only 300 soldiers.

Is Bigger Always Better?

Many times small is sufficient. And sometimes small is significant. Have you noticed how God specializes in overcoming big problems, winning great battles, and showing His awesome power through the smallest of things? No matter how small or inadequate you feel, and no matter how big the challenge, God wants to use you to accomplish significant things for Him.

In this case, God used the #22 size hook of Gideon to defeat the twenty-two-inch army of the Midianites, Amalekites, and others. A little man with an insignificant background, a poor self-image, and big questions about God, Gideon was nevertheless willing to try. And God allowed him to make a big mark in history.

Our abilities and talents are never too small for God to use. He may have a big job for you today, at home, at work, or in a tough relationship. Don't let the size of the problem or the limits of your resources discourage you. After all, God wants our obedience and availability—what little we may have—and He'll provide the rest.

Even though I can't create flies myself, I do enjoy watching a man tying them. He creates tiny emerger flies on #20, #22, and #24 hooks, just as if that's exactly where they'd always belonged. Colored yarn, fine thread, and delicate feathers become masterpieces in skilled and knowing hands—all to create an exact representation of the perfect, living bait.

I know God's hands are crafting me, too. What skill, what wisdom in His work!

FISHING DEEPER
READ MARK 6:35-44

- What little skill, ability, resource, or influence do you have that God can use for His glory?
- When have you felt particularly led by God to help someone in a "small" way that made a "big" difference?

SIX

STRAIGHT AS AN ARROW

FISHING HAS ALWAYS BEEN MY PASSION. BUT MY FRIEND MIKE is an avid hunter. And along with actually stalking his prey, Mike enjoys thinking about, preparing for, and telling stories about his woodsy adventures. Though I've never been a hunter myself, I do appreciate Mike's fascination with the sport.

Like any sport or hobby, though, hunting has certain diminishing returns over the long haul. The excitement wears off a bit. So to add to the challenge and to test his skills at a higher level, Mike took up bow hunting. Failed tries and increased practice led to small successes—and then significant success. In idle conversation, Mike will describe the trophies he has won with the primitive and challenging art of the bow.

One day between church services I asked Mike to tell me about the toughest animal he had ever taken with a bow. "I've never taken the toughest one" he said. "I've tried several times but never got one." Now I'm thinking bear, elk, moose, or mountain lion.

"Alright," I said. "What's the hardest to hit?"

"Fish."

"Fish? What's so tough about a fish?" I queried.

As we talked, Mike explained what I already knew: sending an arrow with power and accuracy is a tough challenge. What

I didn't realize was how powerfully water bends light rays and distorts the action below the surface.

Bow hunting is tough. But launching arrows at fish is a truly daunting challenge.

It's Like Parenting

This is the case with our children, too. (The challenge part, I mean!) The role of a Christian parent is to provide protection, direction, and correction. Not easy. Perhaps that's why Psalm 127:3-4 describes parenting in terms of a warrior with his quiver of arrows.

Sons are a heritage from the Lord, children a reward from him. Like arrows in the hands of a warrior are sons born in one's youth. Blessed is the man whose quiver is full of them.

Why the illustration from archery? Like parenting, it's a very difficult skill to master. It looks easy to those who have never tried it. What could be difficult about putting an arrow on a bow string, pulling it back, and letting it fly? Until you try it, you think you'll hit the bull's eye every time.

In reality, becoming a skilled archer requires training, practice, and patience. And so does parenting. Some of us had the benefit of dads and moms who modeled parenting skills for us. Others were not as fortunate. Today there are many great resources available to help us hone our skills in the challenging arena of parenting.

Solomon, who wrote Psalm 127, chose the image of the warrior for a reason. He could have used the hunter or the sportsman to develop his parenting theme, but he chose the warrior. There is a battle underway for the hearts and minds of our children. The stakes are high and the cost of failure can be fatal. The warrior must protect those who are not yet ready to fight for themselves and provide the secure environment for proper development to take place. We must be warriors for our children, always on the alert, always ready to defend their safe developmental environment. But always with the understanding that we are mentoring and training them to take their place in the battle.

Arrows are delicate and can be damaged easily. They need to be cared for gently to ensure that the head does not become dull, the shaft warped, or that the fletchings do not become crumpled or broken. Without proper protection the effectiveness and the direction of the arrow will be impaired. Most importantly, however, is the nock. This is the small slot at the end of the arrow that connects the arrow to the bow string. Without this point of connection the arrow will not receive the power the archer intends, and it will never travel to its ultimate destination. We must connect with our children. We must make eye contact, give hugs, wrestle on the floor, go fishing, talk in the car, memorize a verse of Scripture, make a puzzle, or exchange a good joke.

Archery requires the arrows to be shot away from the archer. We must send our arrows with power and accuracy to make an impact where we cannot go. Solomon understood the challenge of parenting better than he parented. Within a few weeks of his death, Solomon's son had thrust the nation into civil war, never again to enjoy the power, wealth, and influence it had enjoyed. Solomon had failed to prepare his sons for the challenge of leadership and the nation paid the price.

There are no guarantees for parents. God has given each child a will of his own. The task before us is to guide our children through their developmental years to prepare them for the challenges that lie ahead, wherever they may land.

FISHING DEEPER
READ EPHESIANS 6:4

- Think through the past few months for a moment. Do you have a selfish pattern of behavior or attitude that might have had a negative influence on your children?
- What one thing could you do to enhance the spiritual instruction you are providing your children?

SEVEN

STINGRAY BUFFET

BEAUTIFUL BLUE WATERS SURROUND THE GRAND CAYMAN Island of the western Caribbean. Unlike many of the nearby islands with their majestic volcanic peaks, Grand Cayman is a sleek, low-lying atoll ringed by a coral reef. The beaches of the main island and the breakwater of the reef form the boundaries of a large, crystal-clear bay that reaches depths of ten to fifteen feet.

Years ago, fishermen returned from their day out on the sea and navigated their way through the reef to escape the rough, open waters of the Caribbean. Once inside the reef they cleaned their catch, washed their equipment, and enjoyed the relative calm of the safe harbor.

Over the years scavenger fish recognized the value of feeding below these fishing boats. The food was plentiful, the waters safe. Stingrays, in particular, loved this sheltered feeding ground. Each afternoon they'd come together to enjoy an easy meal while avoiding the harsh open seas.

Staying with the Food

Those fishing boats are long gone, but the stingrays still gather, and the meeting place is now called Stingray City. Even though stingrays don't normally congregate in schools or live in communities, Stingray City is an exception to the rule. Perhaps stingrays somehow understand a basic principle of life: *stay where the food is.*

I find in the Scriptures at least three pictures describing the "feeding habits" of a Christian who wants to grow spiritually strong. First, the apostle Peter used the image of a baby at feeding time to depict the way a young Christian should eagerly drink in all the information available. In 1 Peter 2:2 he writes:

Like newborn babies, crave pure spiritual milk, so that by it you may grow up in your salvation.

A baby's primary challenge is simply to grow. And the only way it can develop properly is to consume a sufficient amount of nutritious food. Similarly, if you are a brand new Christian who desires to grow strong and develop spiritual stamina, you need to receive a steady diet of basic biblical truth.

The second biblical picture is the Lord as the Good Shepherd, who provides green pasture and quiet water for His sheep.

The Lord is my shepherd, I shall not want. He makes me lie down in green pastures, he leads me besides quiet waters. (Psalm 23:1-2)

The feeding frenzy of a "baby Christian" should give way to the consistent grazing of the maturing sheep. Sheep, much like the stingrays, know that the best place to eat is where the food is plentiful. But the key to a sheep eating well is staying near the shepherd and grazing in the green pastures He provides. We, too, need to put ourselves in places where we can receive good teaching and biblical instruction.

The third picture is that of a man sitting down to a meat

and potatoes dinner of solid food. The writer of Hebrews states:

In fact, though by this time you ought to be teachers, you need someone to teach you the elementary truths of God's word all over again. You need milk not solid food. . . . But solid food is for the mature, who by constant use have trained themselves to distinguish good from evil. (Hebrews 5:12,14)

Beyond the milk of basic biblical teaching and the consistent grazing that should be a part of our lives, we must learn to feed ourselves solid meals from God's Word. What would that mean for you in normal, everyday living?

For the stingray, the best feeding occurs in a calm place and during a protected time. Start by carving out a time and place, an inner harbor, free of distraction, in order to enjoy some heavenly fare. For, like the stingray, we can indeed feast on a generous food supply for spiritual growth. Our only requirement is to stay where the food is plentiful—ever so close to the Great Provider, the one of whom it is said: "He is not far from each one of us" (Acts 17:27).

FISHING DEEPER
READ PSALM 119:97-112

- Love is demonstrated in time spent with another. How much time do you spend just being aware of God's presence in your life?
- What kinds of evidence do you see in your life that you are set on doing God's will?

EIGHT

KNOTS

EVERY SUCCESSFUL FISHERMAN KNOWS HOW TO TIE A FEW BASIC knots. That's because fooling a fish requires lots of gizmos and gadgets secured to lines and leader. Connections must be strong to keep essential equipment from separating at the wrong time. Otherwise, a big fish can unravel the line and break off the hook.

Too often I have looked at the end of my fishing rod and seen half an inch of crinkled line with no hook. Then I know there's a nice fish swimming freely with an expensive lure or fly still decorating his lip.

Things come unraveled because of pressure. When there is little pressure, any old knot will do. But when significant pressure hits, and it will, you need knots you can trust.

Spouses: Know Your Knots!

Pressure can stress any relationship. Tension may involve our struggles with money, health, opinions, loyalty, or a host of other issues. And contention can pull us apart, unraveling our relationships, unless we're tied tightly with a knot that won't slip.

Pressure seems to stretch people most dramatically in the relationship of marriage. The potential problems and the resulting trauma can be quite severe when an excessive burden pulls against the marriage knot. Therefore, a few basic relational knots are essential tools for spouses. In every marriage there are times when the line is loaded with strain, when the pressure pulls hard against the knot and we think the union could unravel at any time. So what do you do? Consider these three knots that ought to be in place when the tension mounts:

Commitment. There is a brutal and bizarre story in the book of Judges that centers around a man named Jepthah. He was called by God to lead the Israelites against the Ammonites who threatened Israel's borders. But prior to the big battle Jepthah made a deal with God. Judges 11:30-31 states:

> *And Jepthah made a vow to the Lord: "If you give the Ammonites into my hands, whatever comes out of the door of my house to meet me when I return in triumph from the Ammonites will be the Lord's, and I will sacrifice it as a burnt offering."*

This was a brash, impulsive promise. But there's a noble commitment here, too, and a willingness to follow God no matter the cost.

God did provide a great victory, and Jepthah returned home victorious. The joy of victory quickly turned to terror and heartbreak, however, as his young daughter ran out of the house to meet him.

Reconciling these events with the rest of Scripture's ethic is perplexing, to say the least. But for our purposes, the point is this: the easiest thing for Jepthah would have been to change the rules. He could have rationalized that God wanted him to be happy or that God wouldn't want him to honor a vow he had made in a rash moment. Instead, Jepthah must have known that keeping his word was important to God and critical to his own character. To honor God and to be a person of integrity, he fulfilled his commitment in spite of the painful and traumatic personal cost.

It is possible to have the same kind of commitment in our approach to marriage. But, of course, it won't be easy. For Jepthah, the plans and desires for his daughter's future had no doubt been precious to him. Then everything changed as he experienced the death of those dreams for her future.

Let's make wise and good promises to our mates, and then recognize that following through on our promises may require a sacrifice on our part. If searching for the "convenient" way is our basic approach to life, then our commitment will probably fail; the stress and strain will unravel our marital future.

Communication. Telling our story and hearing the story of our wives is a strong knot that ties us together. Words have meaning. They capture and convey thought for the greatest good. But words can also be horribly destructive. Proverbs 15:1-2 says:

> *A gentle answer turns away wrath, but a harsh word stirs up anger. The tongue of the wise commends knowledge, but the mouth of the fool gushes folly.*

We need to bring gentle words and words of knowledge to our relationship with our wives. Naturally, we'll want to avoid harsh and foolish words that generate pain and embarrassment. We must also ask ourselves: When was the last time we really talked? And how long has it been since I really listened—listened under the surface of the words to hear the feelings that came attached to them?

Christ-centeredness. The third knot is our relationship with God. As we are tied together with loving commitment and deepening communication, the critical final knot is the intertwining of our lives with Christ. Ecclesiastes 4:9-12 speaks of the value of two people facing life's challenges together.

> *Two are better than one, because they have a good return for their work. If one falls down his friend can pick him up. But pity the man who falls and has no one to help him up. Also, if two lie down together, they will keep warm. But how can one keep warm alone? Though one may be over-powered, two can defend themselves. A cord of three strands is not quickly broken.*

Who can deny the benefits of a loyal partnership? But the emphasis here falls on the last line. Three is better than two. A relational knot that includes the third strand of Christ Himself is the strongest bond of all.

Don't let your relationships unravel. Keep them tied tightly. Keep your word, keep talking, and keep the Lord in your midst.

FISHING DEEPER
READ EPHESIANS 5:25-33

- How would your wife know if you were showing her love?
- What is one thing you could do today to let her know how much you love her?

NINE

MID-COURSE CORRECTIONS

LOST LAKE SHIMMERS IN AN EMERALD FOREST OF DOUGLAS fir about halfway between the Columbia River and Mount Hood. The gorgeous view of snow-capped Hood rising from the shores of Lost Lake often appears on postcards and calendars. It's a dramatic testimony to the beauty of Oregon and God's creative majesty.

The lake's peacefulness emanates partly from its majestic setting. But the quiet surroundings also contribute to the entrancing serenity. Bird songs punctuate the stillness, and you can hear voices speaking at normal tones far across the water. No one questions the special rule: Motorboating prohibited!

My older brother Jim, younger brother Paul, and I enjoyed some memorable days fishing Lost Lake as teenagers with our Dad. Rainbow and brook trout were plentiful, and we tried our best to reduce their numbers. I remember setting out one day in our rented wooden rowboat, loaded down with nets, life jackets, cold drinks, and fishing rods. Dad rowed, Paul in the bow trolled directly over his head, while Jim and I extended our rods out each side of the stern. We had a fair first day, catching several twelve-inch fish with flashers, worms, and small silver flatfish lures.

The second day, however, we saw much less action and

had little to show for our several trips around the lake. Nevertheless, at lunch time we were amazed to see a boat pulling up to the dock next to us with a stringer of big ones. How did they do that?

It didn't take us long to learn that our neighbors were simply dragging a spruce fly sixty feet behind the boat and keeping the net handy. So after lunch and a trip to the tackle shop, the fun began for us, too, as eighteen-inch trout attacked our own spruce flies. Fish that had been keepers in the morning were tossed back in the afternoon. By dinner we'd reached our limit and our arms were tired from fighting fish all afternoon.

From Frustration to Success
At first we had worked hard but had little joy or fulfillment. Until we made a small but strategic change in our method.

Success came when we changed our lure. Of course, changing the well-worn patterns and comfortable routines of our lives can be tough—even terrifying. Yet change we must in order to become the people God wants us to be.

Change can make things better but it can also make things worse. Therefore we ought to first consider our current situation and then ask ourselves: *What must I do in these circumstances to improve my character and my effectiveness?*

As we ponder, we can also look to Jesus for some valuable lessons about change. For example, recall the time when He was preparing to teach a crowd of eager listeners along the banks of the Sea of Galilee. The people pressed around Him. He needed a better vantage point to address the crowd. So He borrowed a boat from a fisherman named Simon and began to teach.

Along with his partners, Simon was washing his nets after a tough night out on the water. That morning had been particularly frustrating because he and his friends had fished all night without catching a thing. But Jesus told Simon, "Put out into deep water, and let down the nets for a catch" (Luke 5:4).

At this point, I'd be thinking: *So what does this preaching carpenter know about fishing? It's the wrong time of day, the wrong part of the lake . . . and I just washed my nets!*

Simon complied, though, and hauled in a bursting net full of fish. Then, recognizing his own unworthiness and God's greatness, he cried out: "Go away from me, Lord; I am a sinful man" (Luke 5:8).

Jesus replied, "Don't be afraid; from now on you will catch men" (Luke 5:10). The Lord apparently had bigger and better things in store for Simon. We know that this man would leave his fishing and take up preaching, eventually witnessing a religious wild fire as the Holy Spirit descended to change the world (Acts 2:1-4). Thus the little change that had begun with Simon's reluctant obedience sparked a lifetime of transformation, all of it leading to a work of God that keeps burning brightly to this day.

From Liabilities to Assets

Yes, after his encounter with Jesus some outward changes immediately blossomed in Simon's life. He quickly gave up fishing to become a full-time follower of Christ. His name went from Simon to Peter.

Other changes came slower and were much less visible to those around him. Early in his life Peter was known for his domineering, arrogant manner. Yet at the end of his life God had changed him into a person who wrote, "Humble yourselves, therefore, under God's mighty hand, that he may lift you up in due time" (1 Peter 5:6). Little by little God had taken the liabilities in Peter's life and turned them into valuable assets.

A little change can make a big difference in our lives.

We must become open to change and realize that if we are to grow and improve, we'll need to embrace the new and different. Yes, it's always easier to simply knuckle under to "the way things are." But clinging to the status quo makes improvement impossible.

Perhaps we're in the same rowboat! No doubt, all of us can become more willing to change by loosening our grip a bit on those outdated patterns and stale practices holding us back from a glorious new day, holding us back from becoming the people God wants us to become. In fact, to grow in Christ means always "to be becoming." For it is our sacred calling always to be changing, as the Scripture says, "We all, with open face beholding as in a glass the glory of the Lord, are changed into the same image from glory to glory" (2 Corinthians 3:18, KJV).

FISHING DEEPER
READ MATTHEW 26:36-52 AND 1 PETER 4:7-8

- In what ways have you been like Peter in either of these passages?
- What one little change could you make today to become a better servant of Christ?

TEN

THE ONE THAT GOT AWAY

LOOKING FORWARD TO A FISHING TRIP IS ALMOST AS EXCITING as actually being there. My daydreams are filled with visions of hooking the big one, battling frantically, landing the trophy-sized fish. In my dreams I never get a sunburn, never scratch a mosquito bite, and never let one get away.

I caught a nice size steelhead in Big Creek early in the winter during my senior year in high school. It was a great fish, and it fought a long time in swift water. Every day in school, every Sunday in church, all I thought about was catching another one.

Thus began the Saturday morning ritual. Throughout that winter I got up two hours before sunrise and rode with my two friends some seventy miles to Big Creek. We'd be in the ice-cold water before dawn. My friend Bill often caught some fish. His brother John took home some nice ones, too. But each time I had a strike, the fish got away, and I returned home empty-handed.

My dreams were filled with success; my reality was nothing but failure.

What Is Your Dream?

It seems the dreams of our lives are often like our expectations for a fishing trip. Anticipation fills us with joy and excitement, but we rarely consider the inevitable problems, the potential for pain. We look ahead and expect things to get better. In our mind's eye we get the promotions, our kids do well in school and sports, we move into our dream house, our team wins the championship, and we live long, healthy lives.

After all, why should we bargain on cancer, bankruptcy, divorce, or jail?

In the Bible, we read that Peter was enjoying the Passover dinner with Jesus and the other disciples when the conversation turned to the terrible pain and death that awaited Christ. First, one of the disciples would betray Him. And a dismal denial also loomed ahead:

> *"Simon, Simon, Satan has asked to sift you as wheat. But I have prayed for you, Simon, that your faith may not fail. And when you have turned back, strengthen your brothers." But he replied, "Lord, I am ready to go with you to prison and to death." Jesus answered, "I tell you, Peter, before the rooster crows today, you will deny three times that you know me."* (Luke 22:31-34)

I think Peter fully expected to follow Jesus. But perhaps he saw only the glory and none of the pain. *I will follow you, Jesus . . . to a place of power . . . to the pinnacle of success . . . to lofty heights of happiness.*

Who wouldn't prefer to say it that way—and have it come to pass?

But follow Him to prison and to death? Those weren't Peter's expectations.

They aren't mine either.

It's likely that Peter had envisioned a life of significance, as the world measures it. But in a brief moment, during a night-time prayer meeting in the Garden of Gethsemane, that dream crashed down around him. The pillars propping up his life suddenly crumbled, and he hit the ground hard.

And Peter did deny being a friend of Jesus three times. When the rooster finally crowed, the despair of his failed expectations, coupled with the shame of his denial, left Peter an emotional wreck.

> *Then Peter remembered the word the Lord had spoken to him. . . . And he went outside and wept bitterly.*
> (Luke 22:61-62)

. . . And His Dream?

Yes, any of us can fail. But the great thing about Peter is that he kept coming back. The pain was intense and the problem real, but Peter was unwilling to quit. The other cryptic words of Jesus must have kept rolling around in his head, "When you have turned back, strengthen your brothers." Jesus knew that out of the pain and humiliation Peter would find a new depth in his own life from which he could draw help for others.

Jesus did, however, deal with the problem of superficial daydreaming. Along the Sea of Galilee He and Peter took an early morning walk. Three times Jesus addressed the issues of Peter's love, and after each exchange reaffirming Peter's devotion, Jesus uttered a command: "Feed my sheep." Here Peter was given a new expectation, and from this fresh vision would come the direction for the rest of Peter's life.

Just like the fisherman who comes home empty-handed time and time again, we can be frustrated in our attempts to fulfill our brightest dreams. We may be able to envision a golden future—but we can never produce it.

Our dreams can get away from us.

We can learn to keep coming back, though. We can try again and refuse to give up hope. Out of the failure of Peter's life, God began a process of transformation that took Peter further along the path of true success than even his dreams could carry him.

Is this not the same God who lives in you?

And what dream do you think He has for *your* future?

FISHING DEEPER
READ ACTS 9:1-6, 17-22

- What apparent effect did Paul's persecution of the early church have upon his potential for future service?
- When have you been tempted to think that a failure in your life was so great that God couldn't love or use you?

ELEVEN

RIPPLES

AS EVERY ANGLER KNOWS, IT'S GREAT WHEN YOU CAN ACTUALLY
see the fish before you catch them. But observing fish below
the surface can be challenging. Where the water is crystal-clear
and the surface still—there they are! If the surface is disturbed,
it's tough to distinguish fish from rocks and debris on the bottom.

When the water is even the least bit choppy, seeing the fish
is all but impossible. Nevertheless, every good fisherman
remembers: *Just because I can't see 'em doesn't mean they're not
there.*

Hard to See?
All of this leads me to consider the "flow" of my days, especially
the things I see—and don't see—within them. I know that at
times the waters of my life are calm and crystal-clear. Then
through the stillness I catch glimpses of God and enjoy a view
of his greatness and majesty. But when rippling troubles disturb
my peaceful vision, I may assume that because I can't see Him,
He must not be there.

Several kinds of disturbance create an obscuring, roiling
turmoil in our days. Some of these are beyond our control, but
many are of our own making. First are the disturbances over
which we have little or no control. They blow into our lives,

troubling the quiet stillness we have come to expect. Our health takes a turn for the worse, we lose a job, a close friend seems to betray us. It can be any crisis that has howled across our peaceful pond, disturbing the deep view to which we have grown accustomed. Jesus anticipated such problems when He spoke to His disciples the night before He was crucified:

> *"I have told you these things, so that in me you may have peace. In this world you will have trouble. But take heart! I have overcome the world."* (John 16:33)

When our lives are shattered by problems that hit without warning, and when we feel the pain of being the "innocent party," we can retreat to the peace that is always available through Christ.

The second type of disturbance clouding our view of God is our own fault, the problems of our own making. When I think of all the unwise and thoughtless decisions I've made over the years, I'm hardly surprised they have blurred my perspective on God. Each ill-advised act has created pain for me and often hurt for those around me. Perhaps you, too, have spent money you didn't have, chosen the wrong friends, slept late, eaten too much, watched too much TV, or overloaded your schedule. As we recklessly enter the water, we disturb the serenity God wants us to enjoy. Our poor choices allow tension and embarrassment to seep into our lives, draining the time and energy we need to focus on God. And the little ripples we create as we thrash about cloud our vision of life's goodness.

A third kind of disturbance is simply our blatant sinning. We trouble the water when we allow direct disobedience to permeate our lives. We are controlled by lust, we cheat on our taxes, lie on our résumé, or use anger to intimidate those around us. Instead of backing away from sin and allowing the waters to settle, we often continue to flail around, perhaps adjusting our view of God to accommodate our rebellion. The whole time we are stirring the waters, making it more difficult to see Him with clarity.

Easy to Forget?

When we lose our focus on God, we may question His existence—or at least wonder if He still has any relevance to our daily lives. The ancient Israelites saw God act on their behalf numerous times but quickly forgot the benefits He had provided. Psalm 117:2 says, "For great is his love towards us, and the faithfulness of the LORD endures forever."

When we make a mess of things, how easy it is to forget that God's faithful love endures forever.

I can forget Him when my prayers seem to bounce off the ceiling. I can forget when I go through periods of aching loneliness or crushing anxiety. And, of course, I forget when I'm so mired in my own concerns that the thought of God and His will becomes a major irritation. It's then that God's face hides behind dark clouds.

Yet, through it all, God is here. Not just when things are going well and my needs are satisfied and my wants are met. But even when life's problems, my stupid mistakes, my sinful acts of rebellion make Him less visible to me.

How is it with you?

We all need to open our eyes of faith a bit wider. Become

a little less like Doubting Thomas of the Bible. Take a moment to hear Jesus addressing Thomas' troubled soul when he needed to see more clearly:

> *"Because you have seen me, you have believed; blessed are those who have not seen me and yet believed."*
> (John 20:29)

Thomas—and you and I, too—wanted to walk by sight. The Lord understands that. But it's better to walk by faith.

FISHING DEEPER
READ HEBREWS 11:1-40

- What is your personal definition of "faith"? When have you exercised this type of faith?
- Do the faithful always receive their "reward"? Think through your response by considering a faith event in your own life.

STRIKE INDICATORS

HERE'S MY FORMULA FOR FUN: FRIENDS, BIG TROUT . . . BOTH waiting for me at the San Juan.

New Mexico's San Juan River used to be too warm for trout to survive year round. But since the construction of the Navajo Dam, the river emerges from some three hundred feet below the surface of the reservoir. Water temperature hovers at a constant 38 degrees all year, and the trout love it. The mild climate provides abundant feed throughout the year.

Because the river has been well-managed, lots of big fish, magnificent fighters, thrive in the cool waters. You can catch them by drifting a wet fly along the bottom with the current. The flies resemble the tiny emerging larvae of real-life insects that lay their eggs in the water. As they hatch, these bugs emerge from the bottom of the river, rise through the water, and escape into the air. During this transition from bottom-dwelling larvae to free-flying insects, they become lunch for the already over-stuffed trout.

But how does one monitor the tiny manmade fly as it drifts along the bottom?

That's where the strike indicator comes in. The most common type is a frayed ball of waterproof yarn attached between the fly line and the leader. This hairy mass of tangled threads floats on top of the water, as though standing on tiny legs, and moves with the flow of the river. It remains motionless as long as the fly is also moving with the current. Any twitch or movement of the yarn announces activity below the surface. And the watchful fisherman knows: time to set the hook.

Looking Below

Much goes on below the surface of a river—and below the outer layers of any human life. Consider Saul, for instance, the first king of ancient Israel. Saul was the obvious choice to be king, from all outward appearances. Strong, tall, and distinguished, he came from a respectable family. Just the kind of powerful leader that could bring the Hebrew tribes together to defend their borders.

As king, Saul received special instructions before a crucial battle with the Amalekites. The directive appeared harsh. He was to take no prisoners and he must destroy all enemy property. After the victory Saul obeyed generally but not completely. He spared the life of the enemy king, and he took some of the choice animals (under the pretense of saving them for a special sacrificial offering).

So what do we find when we look below the surface of Saul's life? Though he was kingly in appearance, his character was flawed, his heart disobedient. Because Saul was unwilling to obey God completely, he lost the privilege of leadership for himself and his descendants.

Samuel, the high priest, was commanded to anoint a new king. So, in the small town of Bethlehem, at the home of a man named Jesse, Samuel considered several brothers, the oldest and most distinguished being Eliab.

> *Samuel saw Eliab and thought, "Surely the Lord's anointed stands here before the Lord." But the Lord said to Samuel, "Do not consider his appearance or his height, for I have rejected him. The Lord does not look at the things man looks at. Man looks on the outward appearance, but the Lord looks at the heart." (1 Samuel 16:6-7)*

Certainly Eliab had his strong points. And the youngest and least kingly of Jesse's sons met none of the world's expectations for kingship. But David was excellent material for kingship: "a man after God's own heart" (1 Samuel 13:14).

Even on a very small résumé, could anything look better than that?

Seeing What's There

Do you tend to see what people are really like, below the surface? Your interpersonal "strike indicator" is your ability—and *responsibility*—to look much deeper than outward appearances. God calls you to do it because the facade of a life seldom reveals the soul within.

Unfortunately, we tend to be oblivious to the real quality of a person's character. What can we do? First, we can stop assuming that the hearts of our friends and neighbors are as peaceful and pure as they appear in public. Second, we can avoid judging a person's character based on first impressions: young, old, rich, poor, masculine, feminine . . . Go ahead, add a few of your own favorite snap-judgment criteria:

61

-
-
-
-
-
-
-

None of these things matters very much. Because the quality of a man's character depends largely upon this: *Does his heart beat in sync with the heart of God?*

The standard by which we evaluate others may act as a special kind of strike indicator, demonstrating to us what we truly value. That standard may tell us more about ourselves than we want to know. Too often we make the mistake of Samuel and judge solely according to looks.

Suppose, instead, we saw people with the eyes of God?

FISHING DEEPER
READ PSALM 147:10-11

- In your opinion, what things put a smile on the face of God?
- Do you think you've been able to make God smile lately? How?

FISHING FOR LIFE

WE SPORT FISHERMEN SPEND A LOT OF TIME THINKING about . . . fishing. So whenever we get the chance to pursue our beloved hobby, our senses go on high alert. Most of us are eager enough to get up early, skip lunch, endure freezing temperatures, and ignore scorching sunburns. The problems and pain don't seem to matter much in light of the potential reward. After all, we're talking *pure bliss!*

Ever met a professional fishermen? I've known only a few, and they're the envy of the rest of us. While we're dreaming about getting out of the office and away from the job, they're out on the water enjoying a most heavenly pursuit.

And the pros I've known seemed to enjoy going to work every morning. But I sometimes wonder whether professionals ever feel the temptation to take it all for granted—the beauty that always surrounds them, the fine gear they get to use, the big fish they constantly hold in their hands.

Becoming calloused to the thrill of the catch? Tough for me to imagine. For the professional, though, maybe fishing is just another day at the office.

Danger Here!
They say familiarity breeds contempt. I'm quite certain it could

happen with fishing. But what about with spiritual things?

I think we Christians live with two dangers. The first is, indeed, the hazard of becoming too like the professional fisherman, whose familiarity with his vocation can dull him to the thrill of the experience. The "professional Christian" might be the man who sees God working in his life and in the lives around him but over time loses the excitement. Maybe he trades his initial wonder at God's work for a more academic, reserved response over the long haul.

Sadly, this can easily happen to those of us in full-time ministry. We were drawn into ministry because of our excitement about what God was doing in our lives. He had saved us and changed us. And we wanted to be a part of what God was doing in the lives of others. However, years of committee meetings, potluck suppers, counseling sessions, correspondence, and irate phone calls left us long on technique and short on zeal.

Yes, it happens: becoming so familiar with the things of God that we begin taking them for granted. When we become calloused to His benefits we lose our focus on Him. We forget Christ's agony, which provided our grace. We neglect the core of our lives, which connects us with Him. We trade glimpses of His grandeur for absorption with busyness. Our awe of God is exchanged for activity; meaning gives way to method, and passion loses out to position. To fight against this potential problem we must focus on all that God has provided for us. The psalmist reminds us: "Praise the Lord, O my soul, and forget not all his benefits" (Psalm 103:2).

Advertising specialists distinguish between features and benefits. Features are the bells and whistles of an item, things like size, color, and functions. But benefits emphasize the results that a buyer will receive from owning the item. Benefits describe *what the item will do for you.* The catalog may list the features of a fly rod as eight feet long, four sections, and made of graphite. But the benefit is on the full-color cover: the smiling face of the fisherman who's holding a twenty-inch trout.

Features answer the *what?* Benefits answer the *why?*

Focusing on the benefits helps us keep our relationship with God lively and full of expectancy. We remember that God has made us a junior partner with Him in changing the world. We're not just going to meetings, we're joining Him in exciting work. We can begin to sense God's strength around us as the battle rages and victories are won. Thy kingdom come, Thy will be done is the *why* of everything we can see and touch. With such a perspective, how could we become numb to the privilege before us?

That brings us to the second danger we face as Christians. It's dreaming about fishing, talking about fishing, planning to go fishing, but never leaving the office to actually get out to the water.

Always dreaming, never doing.

Excuses come easy for us sport fishermen when we ought to move from planning to participation. Our schedule is too crowded; no one will cover for us. Thus we avoid eye contact, move quickly to the exit, or fail to return phone calls. We live like the characters in the parable of the Good Samaritan. They saw a need but chose to stay on schedule while missing a chance to demonstrate godly love and concern.

The reason: it's easier to be a dreamer than a doer.

Do This!

But enough of what *not* to do. Here are two simple suggestions that can help any of us avoid both dangers and remain fresh in God's work. First, keep doing what you are doing right now. Take time each day to refresh yourself with lessons and principles from God's Word. The writer of Psalm 119:103 says,

> *How sweet are your words to my taste,*
> *sweeter than honey to my mouth!*

Not only are the words pleasant but they also provide a burst of energy. God's Word gives us the energy to move from being a dreamer to being a doer.

Second, take time away to recoup your emotional and spiritual resources. We need what writer Richard Swenson calls "margins" in our lives. Do you have any time in your days for just thinking, praying, reflecting, praising, and evaluating your progress? If not, the peril is great because growth in the spiritual life is more than a sport and bigger than any profession. If we lose interest in this one thing . . . don't we risk losing everything else?

FISHING DEEPER
READ 1 KINGS 19:1-18

- Why was Elijah discouraged? What steps did God use to restore Elijah to a place of active service?
- How have you handled your own discouraging times? How would you like to handle them?

FOURTEEN

MUD IN YOUR EYE

IN ONE OF MY EARLIEST MEMORIES I CAN STILL SEE DAD AND Grandpa returning from a day of fishing at Nehelm Bay. They're holding a heavy stringer of flounder and sea perch. The flounders' grotesque eyes fascinated me because both eyes stare out of the same side of their contorted heads. Those fish were strange when I was five years old, and at forty-five I still can't quite fathom why they look the way they do.

I do know that when a flounder is born, his eyes are on opposite sides of his head. But soon one eye begins to migrate to join the other. Eventually both eyes are functioning on the same side. Strange, isn't it?

But there's a reason for it. You see, adult flounder lie on their sides on the bottom of the ocean, with both eyes looking upwards into the water above. If it wasn't for the migrating eye, one eye would always point down into the mud and one would be open to the fresh water above.

Would that be any way to live—having one eye in the mud for a lifetime?

Spending Your Time . . . *Where?*

When a person spends too much time in the mud something needs to give. But not just any old change will do. When we spend time in the filth of this world we have a tendency to let our values migrate over time. The subtle accommodation occurs as we adjust our standards just a bit lower.

Maybe that's what happened to Samson. He was a special child, born to a couple who'd longed for a son. But his parents were given specific commands as to how he should be raised. He must never drink wine; he must avoid anything dead or unclean; he must never cut his hair. Samson's superhuman strength depended on following these regulations to the letter.

All of this because Samson had a special mission in life. His purpose was to deliver Israel from the enemy Philistines. His problem, as you know, was that he started enjoying the company of Philistines — one in particular. He had visited the Philistine city of Timnah and was smitten by a beautiful young woman there. Instead of following God's directive to marry only within the Israelite nation, he demanded his way. He told his parents, "I have seen a Philistine woman in Timnah; now get her for me as my wife" (Judges 14:2).

While on the way to arrange for his marriage, Samson was attacked by a lion, which he killed with his bare hands. When he returned for his wedding he found that bees had built a hive in the carcass of the lion. Samson reached into the lion and scooped out the honey, violating his responsibility to avoid contact with any dead body. Later in a conflict with the Philistines he picked up the jawbone of a donkey and killed a thousand men. Once again he disregarded the divine command to avoid touching the dead.

Finally, he revealed to his lover, Delilah, the secret of his great strength. As a result, he lost his hair and he lost his power.

The Philistines captured him, gouged out his eyes, and forced him to work like an ox to amuse them.

What a sad turn of events for one of such promise.

Don't Get Comfortable Down There

Samson compromised his standards and adjusted his ethics to the point of losing everything that had once made him successful. Little by little his eyesight had migrated to a place that was comfortable for him. But there he was unable to see the true danger of his situation.

Of course, he had lost his spiritual sight long before he lost his physical eyesight. For the migration in his life was a move in reverse. He was not as the flounder, whose eye moves away from the mud. Rather, his vision settled back to the bottom.

Yet, graciously, God allowed Samson's hair to grow back and allowed his strength to return. In a moment of amusement the Philistines brought their old enemy out of his prison cell to make fun of him at their party. While in the Philistine temple Samson dislodged the pillars supporting the roof. He died with his enemies when the roof came crashing down upon them all. Thus one of the saddest obituaries in the Bible appears in Judges 16:30: "He killed many more when he died than while he lived."

Quite an accomplishment for a man who had every opportunity life could provide.

But how hard should we come down on Samson? I, too, know how comfortable it can be in the mud. Have you been there, lately? While we're feeding our addictions, we take away all the rough edges. We can sink down into fantasy, escape into a numbing softness. What is it for you that brings a little mind-less, short-term fulfillment to the day? Think: How long can you keep going back to that spot before the silt begins to choke out your spiritual life?

My advice: don't snuggle up in the mud. Be sensitive to the choices you're making and the impact those choices are having on your life. Check yourself to see if you are changing. And ask: in which direction?

It's too easy to get cozy while changing for the worse.

FISHING DEEPER
READ ROMANS 1:21-32

- What is the starting point for the sinful deterioration high-lighted in these verses?
- In what areas of your life do you need to glorify God or give Him thanks?

FIFTEEN

SHARKS

AT THE RIPE OLD AGE OF TWENTY-THREE MY FATHER FOUND himself second in command of the LST 601, embroiled in the Mediterranean action of WWII. The awkward looking LST with blunt-bow landed soldiers and tanks on hostile shores. Several smaller landing craft, attached to the LST, deposited the Marines into the teeth of enemy resistance.

After a tour of the Mediterranean, the 601 returned to the U.S. by way of precommunist Cuba. The stop provided an opportunity for some much needed rest and training. During their stay, the sailors amused themselves by taking the landing craft for test rides while fishing for giant sharks which infested the waters near their berth. A piece of meat on a makeshift hook created great trolling. Sharks are the tigers of the sea and they proved it time and time again by attacking the fresh meat with ferocity—delighting the young sailors of the 601.

Learn from the Shark

It's true; all sharks are rather strange, unique creatures in many respects. They have no bones, for example, just cartilage. They only grow as big as their environment allows. And, perhaps most amazing of all, sharks can't breathe unless they're moving forward.

As peculiar as they are, sharks and their unique characteristics can teach us some lessons about Christian living. First is the lesson of flexibility. The strength and power of the shark stems from its flexible makeup, the supple cartilage that can twist and bend with the demands of its muscles. Yet many of us Christians lose power and become ineffective because of reduced flexibility.

Actually, some Christians seem to enjoy rigidity for the sake of being rigid. They dig in and hold positions that have little to do with the truth of God's Word. They bicker and squabble over issues that have little bearing on eternity. Christianity, for them, becomes a list of petty do's and dont's that keeps everyone focused on the surface issues of life.

The apostle Paul stood firm on critical issues of theology and ethics. For example, he once rebuked Peter regarding an ethical issue that had theological implications (Galatians 2:11-21).We might say that Paul was rigid on critical issues of truth and yet flexible in methodology. He explained it this way:

> *To the weak I became weak, to win the weak. I have become all things to all men so that by all possible means I might save some. I do all this for the sake of the gospel.* (1 Corinthians 9:22-23)

Paul apparently knew which issues were worth fighting for and which were simply matters of preferred style among believers. He was versatile in his own style of ministry so that he could interact with as many people as possible. He built bridges through his lifestyle and avoided building walls so that all people could accept the good news he offered. Becoming inflexible in the light of our Christian freedom walls us off from ministry opportunities.

The second thing we can learn from sharks is the lesson of environment. The shark grows to the size of his world—and gets no bigger. Christians may also limit their spiritual growth to the size of their environment. In 2 Corinthians 5:20 Paul says, "We are therefore Christ's ambassadors." Ambassadors live in one country but their real home is elsewhere. They reside in a place where they are responsible to carry out special duties on behalf of their homeland. However, their identity is wrapped up in the land of their citizenship.

Have you ever felt as though you were losing sight of the homeland? Our true citizenship is in heaven, but that is easy to forget. If we focus only on the issues of this world, we will grow to the limits it places upon us. If, on the other hand, we realize that our passport comes from heaven, and we grasp the immense proportions of our true habitat, we will be able to grow and develop far beyond the limits of this world.

Third is the lesson of progress. A shark's breathing apparatus becomes inoperable when he is not moving forward. He needs to stay constantly on the move if he is to survive. We Christians are like that, too, constantly needing to move forward so that we won't be satisfied with the status quo. Ronald Reagan defined the status quo as, "The mess we're in." And we can get comfortable in our "mess," rather than moving forward and making a difference. Then the apostle's attitude can encourage us:

Forgetting what is behind and straining toward what is ahead, I press on toward the goal to win the prize for

which God has called me heavenward in Christ Jesus.
(Philippians 3:13-14)

I know I need to keep moving, even when I feel inadequate or frightened by what could loom ahead. Because, just as it is for the shark, resting can be deadly.

FISHING DEEPER
READ DANIEL 6:1-22

- Remember that Daniel was about eighty years old at this time. What qualities made Daniel a great ambassador?
- What could you do to make these qualities a part of your own life?

SIXTEEN

FIREHOLE RIVER

THIS SUMMER WOULD BE DIFFERENT — THE SUMMER OF 1964, when I turned twelve years old.

Oh, for years I'd been fishing the back waters of the Columbia or Willamette rivers. And occasionally Dad and I would head out to the lakes of the Cascade Mountains. But this year the family station wagon was rolling east into the heart of the Rockies — to Yellowstone National Park.

Our big green Rambler, with push-button automatic transmission, ate up the miles along the Columbia River, through Idaho, into Jackson Hole, Wyoming, through the Tetons, and into the most majestic park I'd ever seen. Sure, I'd glimpsed some pictures and heard stories about Yellowstone: towering mountains, Old Faithful, bubbling mud pots, thundering waterfalls, and roaming black bears. But I was especially intrigued by the stories of the fish in the Firehole River.

Often in life, when expectations run high, the actual event is disappointing. But not Yellowstone. Like the Queen of Sheba encountering Solomon's wealth and wisdom, I could say that "the half had not been told." Seeing this natural treasure for the first time, I imagined myself as Jim Bridger or one of the early explorers. The unique landscape captivated me, inspiring even a twelve-year-old with the magnificence of creation.

It didn't take me long to get my fly rod assembled and begin my quest for trout. I fished first in a wide stream that meandered through an open meadow lined with pine and scrub oak. My family sat in the shade on the bank as I began my conquest.

Moments later I looked up to find a herd of thirty to forty elk staring at me from the opposite side of the stream. I was more curious than frightened because they seemed to belong, and I felt at home as well. My parents, however, wisely decided that the Bolin herd should return to the Rambler.

Our next attempt was on the famous Fishing Bridge. It was a mad house. Hundreds of people lined the sides of the roadway, most with brand new fishing poles, more interested in posing for photos than catching fish. That was no place for a serious, experienced fisherman, and I didn't stay there long.

By this time my siblings had invested all the vacation they could afford in their brother's desire to land a trout. Dad, however, wanted me to catch at least one fish. So he drove me to a remote part of the Firehole, and I began to try again.

Cast after cast resulted in nothing. I was undaunted, but Dad knew time was running short. "I'd give fifty cents to see that line straighten out with a fish on it," he said. The words were still echoing across the water when a rainbow hit my fly and came up out of the water. I played him into my net and returned to our campsite satisfied that I had fulfilled my quest.

Both Fathers Want Our Best
I think Dad wanted me to catch that fish more than I did. But that's exactly the way a father ought to be. In the Sermon on the Mount in Mathew 7:9-11 Jesus says,

Which of you, if his son asks for bread, will give him a stone? Or if he asks for a fish, will give him a snake? If you, then, though you are evil, know how to give good gifts to your children, how much more will your Father in heaven give good gifts to those who ask him!"

Dad couldn't actually give me a fish, but he gave me the opportunity to catch one, and he provided the necessary equipment. His desire was for me to realize my dream and to accomplish my goal, but only if it was in my best interest. He moved me away from fishing when danger approached and when the surroundings weren't conducive to authentic fishing.

Our heavenly Father wants the very best for us, and I believe He wants it even more than we do. We want our way; God wants our best. We see a part; God sees the whole. We barely understand the present; God knows the future.

I'm heartened by all of this. I can bring my requests to God, knowing that He wants the best for me. And I know that any answer He gives will surpass my feeble expectations.

He is wise enough to use *His* definition of success, not mine.

FISHING DEEPER
READ MATTHEW 6:5-13

- How many times is the word "Father" used in these verses?
- When you pray, do you feel as though you are talking to a loving father? How does this help you?

HOOKED ON FISHING

MASON, MY BIG TOMCAT, WAS ONE TOUGH CUSTOMER. TOTALLY
black except for the pink of his nose and the insides of his
ears, his vaccination records named me his owner. But we both
knew he was master of his kingdom: a 125-acre children's
summer camp where I served as director. Mason was every
child's best friend, though. Especially when that child sneaked
him a morsel of food from the dining room.

During most of the year Mason spent his days hunting
mice. But during the summer months, his focus turned to
fishing. In the afternoons he would lie on a wooden bridge
spanning the fishing pond separating the boys' and girls' cabins.
Here Mason watched as the children tempted fish with leftover breakfast sausage. The inhabitants of the little one-acre
pond were perch, about the size of a camper's hand, and a few
big catfish. The policy was strictly catch and release.

One sunny, hot Texas day a cloud of dust with a camper
inside came swirling towards me screaming something about
a crisis by the bridge. It seems Mason had become too well
acquainted with a freshly caught perch and now found himself
with a #4 hook through his upper lip.

At first he didn't want me to come near, but he soon let me
pet him and eventually hold him. I was able to calm him and

78

keep him relatively controlled. The children, of course, were another story. They gathered around to watch the curious adventure of the camp director, his cat, and the #4 hook.

The calm in Mason's demeanor ended when I touched the hook, triggering the tiger instincts deep within him. He was out of my grasp and through the ring of children before you could say *humane society.*

After treating the scratches on my own arms and legs, I tracked Mason down and convinced him to go for a ride in my yellow 1968 MGB. We conveniently ended up at the veterinarian's office, and in a few minutes the hook was clipped and normalcy was restored.

Three Hooks—Even Worse!

While I was emptying my wallet, the vet told me about a hound dog that had experienced a problem similar to Mason's. But instead of a single #4 hook, the dog had encountered a bass plug with triple hooks. One hook lodged in the dog's lip, and a second snagged one of his forepaws as he fought to get the first hook out. The final hook grabbed his hind leg as he tried to scratch out the first two. Three hooks had captured the poor beast. He was incapacitated and in significant pain.

My thinking about hooks and animals moves me to consider our own human vulnerability to lacerating barbs of temptation. Three razor-sharp hooks would love to inflict pain in our lives and render us ineffective for Christ. I John 2:15-16 says:

> *If anyone loves the world the love of the Father is not in him. For everything in the world—the cravings of sinful*

man, the lust of his eyes and the boasting of what he has and does—comes not from the Father but from the world.

In this passage, "world" refers to rebellion against God . It takes us prisoner with a three-part attack: the hook of inordinate passion—our consuming cravings; the hook of possessions—the lusting of our eyes; and the hook of prestige—our pride in what we own and accomplish.

Each of us has felt the sting of these soul-wounding barbs. We often want what is not ours. We acquire more and more as our dissatisfaction with what we have continues to escalate. We strive to find a place in the limelight, based on what we have or what we can do. The hooks snag us and hold us.

The pain of the hook was immediate for the cat and dog. But there is a time delay with the hooks that pierce and hold us. We can become oblivious to the pain until after the hook is set and our ability to resist drains away.

Each of us faces at least one hook ready to snag us every day. But we can only become hooked when we get too close to our "favorite" temptation—the one that has an uncanny capacity to strike at our character's weakest point.

What is it for you? How far away do you need to keep from the bakery, the storefront window, or another man's wife? What is waiting to capture your eyes, your heart, your soul?

FISHING DEEPER
READ ROMANS 12:1-2

- How is the world trying to conform you to it these days?
- What could you do that would help renew your mind?

EIGHTEEN

FAMILY PORTRAIT

ON MY OFFICE WALL HANGS A FAMILY PORTRAIT. IT'S NICELY framed and remains under a protective glass to ensure its safety and longevity. My wife had it framed for me on my forty-fourth birthday as an expression of her love and support. Everyone in the picture is facing the same direction, arranged in nice, straight rows, but each member of the family is unique.

Yet they all are marked by a distinguishing family similarity. Some live in the east and some in the west, some are bigger than others and some more colorful than the rest. But no matter their background or situation in life, there's no denying the family resemblance. My wife's ninety-nine-year-old grandmother has an expression about this striking family likeness. She says: "They favor."

What Kind of Family?

I guess I should tell you that it is not the Bolin family but the Trout family that hangs on my wall. I'm looking at Rainbows and Brookies, Dolly Varden and Browns. Each fish is unique but each one carries the trout family resemblance.

We are all part of a human family, but if we have put our trust in Christ, we are a part of God's family as well. Each member of the family is unique but each carries the family

81

likeness. And as children of God we'll "favor" our Father and reflect to those around us a striking portrait of His character.

Specifically, what are the distinguishing marks of God's children? What supersedes our differences and clearly states to the world that we are family with Jesus? Certain distinguishing marks of God's family members come through in chapter two of 1 John. First, each member exercises obedience:

We know that we have come to know him if we obey his commands. The man who says, "I know him," but does not do what he commands is a liar, and the truth is not in him. But if anyone obeys his word, God's love is truly made complete in him. (verses 3-5)

We Christians have been given some very clear directives about how to please our Father. He imposes rules, but not to limit our fun and make life miserable. Rather, such guidelines make life more enjoyable and help us avoid pain. We distinguish ourselves as family members when we conform our actions, our thoughts, and even our attitudes to God's design.

The second distinguishing feature of God's family members is the mark of love. 1 John 2:9 says,

Anyone who claims to be in the light but hates his brother is still in darkness. Whoever loves his brother lives in the light.

The surest way to test a person's rightful place in God's family is to check on how well he gets along with his "siblings" in the church. In the Christian family, God puts a premium on the kids getting along. Sometimes Christian brothers and sisters do disagree. But the differences of opinion can stay focused on the issues, and siblings can avoid personal attack and vindictiveness. If we harbor ongoing animosity toward another member of God's family we must address the situation and quickly restore our fellowship.

The third feature that sets apart members of God's family is their desire to abide in Christ and to walk closely with Him.

> *And now, dear children, continue in him, so that when he appears we may be confident and unashamed before him at his coming.* (1 John 2:28)

When I was a child, the big event of the day was Dad coming home from work. We all looked forward to hearing the station wagon accelerating up the street and turning into the driveway. Most afternoons I eagerly awaited Dad's return.

Some days, however, I wasn't excited to see the car, and I got a sinking feeling when it turned into the driveway. On those days I had been disobedient towards Mom or gotten into a fight with my sister or brothers.

When I obeyed my mother and when there was harmony with my siblings, I enjoyed a positive relationship with my father. When disobedience or disharmony entered the picture, the relationship became strained and difficult, not because my father had changed but because I had practiced some un-family-like behaviors. Of course, Dad was always ready to restore the relationship, but when I dishonored the family portrait, I lived with inner tension and shut myself off from him.

I realize that all of this applies to me even now, as I start another new day in the family of God. And throughout this day I hope to live like a child of my Father. Perhaps I'll learn a bit more about what it means, in practical terms, to conform myself to His image as I face my problems—the significant worries and the tiny irritations. Maybe I'll take up an opportunity to show my world that I carry the distinguishing marks of the Christian family.

Obedience to God's commands and harmony with God's children pave the way for an ongoing relationship with God Himself. Commit yourself to reflecting God's likeness among everyone you will meet today.

FISHING DEEPER
READ LUKE 20:21-25

- Why did Jesus end with the words, "and to God, what is God's"?
- In what ways are you showing your friends that you carry God's genetic makeup?

NINETEEN

AT THE CROSSROADS

THE APRIL SUN SHONE BRIGHTLY, BUT A COLD WIND BIT INTO my face and the river ran high, fast, and icy outside Buena Vista, Colorado. I crossed a footbridge and walked upstream until I found a pool wrapping around a large boulder jutting into the current. Something told me big fish would be feeding in the quiet, shadowy water near the rock.

For the better part of an hour I fished with flies, eggs, and lures. I fished shallow and I fished deep; I fished close to the boulder and away from the boulder. I just knew fish were waiting for me, but I couldn't prove it. Having exhausted this prime fishing hole (as well as my patience), I drove a mile or so upstream and explored a new stretch of water. The rest of the day provided better results, not great results, but at least I got the smell of fish on my hands.

In the middle of the afternoon I returned to the bridge in time to see three young boys fishing my original hole by the big boulder. *They're wasting their time in that spot,* I thought as I tried to decide whether to head upstream, downstream, or back to my room. Just then, one of the boys had a strike. I watched him play the fish and land a twenty-inch rainbow. I was a little surprised and a little embarrassed that the youngster had done what I couldn't. But when one of the other boys lifted their stringer, I counted five big trout. Now I was ticked! Those should have been my fish. I was there first!

What did they know that I didn't?

That final fish may have satisfied their angling desires or, more likely, their mothers wanted them home before dinner. But for some reason they gathered their things, packed their gear, and headed home with their stringer of big trout. "Nice catch," I managed to blurt as they walked past. I quickly moved back into the spot they had vacated, rigged my outfit, and began to fish.

I tried an assortment of lures, eggs and flies, and finally, just before sundown, I landed a big fish. After I sat on him twice, he measured twenty inches. I was rejoicing, but I felt a little empty and incomplete. I wanted someone to say, "Nice catch," and really mean it. I wanted people to cheer and tell my parents that their son was a great fisherman and that he had caught a great fish. But no one was there to cheer me up or cheer me on. In my moment of triumph I had no one to share my joy.

Enough Blessing for Everyone?

The Bible tells us to "rejoice with those who rejoice" (Romans 12:15). I think this is crucial because the extent of our ability to rejoice with others is a thermometer-reading of our spiritual temperature. If we are able to hear of God's blessing upon someone else and be truly excited for him and his good fortune, then we have moved closer to Christian maturity. If we can see a friend hold up a stringer of blessings that God has provided— and realize that there are lots more blessings in the river— then we have begun to see life from God's perspective.

Why is that so hard? I find it easy to be enthusiastic when

telling others of my blessings, but I tend to feel left out as I listen to their various benefits, advantages, and profits. I become jealous, wondering why these things haven't happened to me.

Maybe I'm thinking that somehow God has a limited number of blessings and that when He gives a great gift to someone else it decreases my chance of obtaining some special favor down the road. Yet there is no scarcity when it comes to God's blessings. His abundance isn't diminished when He gives graciously to those around me.

Surely, if we are to grow in faith, we will go through times when the fish don't bite at all. Or our stringer is not as full as our friends'.

I'm beginning to see that each time I hear of God's goodness toward another I stand at a crossroads. Will I complete my friend's joy and enter into his celebration? Or will I begrudge him the excitement and wrongly assume that his happiness comes at my expense?

FISHING DEEPER
READ PHILIPPIANS 4:4

- What in your life moves you to rejoice today?
- What, in the life of a friend, *should* make you rejoice today?

TWENTY

BIRD'S NEST TANGLES

DISORGANIZED, DYSFUNCTIONAL, DISGUSTING LINES RUNNING in every direction, commanding your attention while the fish are jumping all around you.

Tangles.

What could be more exasperating? You're on the water, the fish are biting. And there you sit, desperately trying to bring order to a bird's-nest jumble of nylon.

No matter his skill level or experience, every fisherman deals with tangles. They attack the reel, ensnare the tip of the pole, snarl the lures. The greatest joy of all are the tangles involving the stranger to your right when your cast drifts too far in his direction. Then the great, unwritten law of fishing kicks in: "The size and difficulty of your tangle will be in direct proportion to: (1) how well the fish are biting, and (2) the number of people watching."

How Do You Handle the Tangles?

Obviously, tangles can mess up more than fishing lines. The relationships in our lives often become tangled, too. They become complicated and tense as order and structure give way to boiling emotions and hurt feelings. When such complications occur, we need to know how to respond.

Some of us have the gift of making a bad situation worse. We add pressure by pulling in our direction and the tangled web becomes more constricted. As the knot tightens, the possibility of a simple solution quickly disappears. Words that blame, accuse, embarrass, or insult add tension. Acts that isolate, demean, shame, or hurt create pressure that makes the unraveling process nearly impossible.

On the other hand, many of us immediately pull out the knife and start cutting. We prefer to cut the other person out of our life and start over, rather than endure the pain of personal confrontation. However, even after such painful relational surgery, the problem remains. We've only moved it aside in order to bypass it for awhile. The hurt is unresolved, growth has not occurred, and we have established a destructive pattern for the future.

I'd like to suggest a better approach for resolving a relational snarl: avoid adding tension. We all know that pulling on a tangle only makes it worse. Loosening it is generally the best method of getting a better view of the problem; it also gives you room to work. So take steps to relax the situation. Make room for putting the lines of communication back in their proper places. Here's how Jesus put it in His Sermon on the Mount:

> *"Therefore, if you are offering your gift at the altar and there remember that your brother has something against you, leave your gift there in front of the altar. First go and be reconciled to your brother; then come and offer your gift."* (Matthew 5:23-24)

Notice that the instruction here speaks to the offending party—the one who has done the tangling. His responsibility is to make the first step in restoring the relationship. Later in the book of Matthew, Jesus says,

"If your brother sins against you, go and show him his fault, just between the two of you. If he listens you have won your brother over." (Matthew 18:15)

This time Jesus puts the initiating responsibility on the one who has been offended. The formula is therefore all-encompassing. If you are in a tangled relationship, it is your responsibility to initiate reconciliation, no matter who started the problem or whose fault it is.

Of course, humbling ourselves and admitting we've hurt someone isn't easy. And it's even harder to lay aside our resentment toward a person who has hurt us. Whatever the cause, though, the first step of loosening the tangle is to stop pulling and start talking.

FISHING DEEPER
READ MATTHEW 18:21-35

- Who do you need to forgive in the coming days?
- Is there anyone you need to ask for forgiveness?

TWENTY-ONE

WINTER KILL

SLOGGING UP STEEP, ROCKY TRAILS. THE SWEAT POURING DOWN under a mammoth backpack. Blisters swelling beneath wool socks and heavy leather boots. . . .

The best of times, the worst of times. Maybe you, too, have tried reaching the high lakes of Oregon's Cascade Range. Yes, they've got some great trout fishing. But reaching those crystal-clear, snow-fed gems requires a couple days of significant effort. Only serious fishermen are willing to do it.

By studying a geological survey map, a committed fisherman can locate lakes off the beaten path. With a map, compass, and a little common sense, adventure lovers can take their chances, visions of huge fish spurring them on.

The lakes without marked trails tend to be small and a long way from the major pathways. But here's the bigger problem: if the fish were in these lakes, earlier fishermen would have created trails and by now those waters would be more accessible. In other words, the reason most have no trails is because they have no fish.

Why no fish? Winter-kill. Trout love cold water, but too cold is *too cold*. These shallow lakes freeze solid in winter, killing any fish that may have migrated into them or may have been stocked during the summer.

Shallow water is deadly to fish when the cold winds blow.

Beware the Shallows!

Without deep water insulated by a thick layer of surface ice, fish will be vulnerable and die. Similarly, a kind of depth is critical in the spiritual life. Especially if we are to have a place of refuge when the world turns icy cold. The superficial Christian life is great when the sun shines and all is well, but when problems come — and they will — the safe place is in a deep relationship with God. Jesus tells a parable about all of this:

> *"A farmer went out to sow his seed. As he was scattering the seed, some fell along the path, and the birds came and ate it up. Some fell on rocky places, where it did not have much soil. It sprang up quickly, because the soil was shallow. But when the sun came up, the plants were scorched, and they withered because they had no root. Other seed fell among thorns, which grew up and choked the plants. Still other seed fell on good soil, where it produced a crop — a hundred, sixty or thirty times what was sown."* (Matthew 13:3-8)

Fortunately, Jesus explains the parable and gives a detailed account of what keeps the seeds from going deep and growing tall. Why not read the rest of the chapter, through verse 23, in your Bible right now? You'll see that the first growth hindrance is a lack of understanding (verse 19). Without basic understanding a person will remain shallow and vulnerable to the attacks of the devil. Second are troubles and persecution (verse 21). With no deep roots a person may appear stable, but in reality he lacks an adequate source of nourishment and refreshment. As the heat rises, he withers.

Third are the worries of this life and the deceitfulness of wealth (verse 22). These can choke and squeeze the life from a person who has begun to grow but fails to withstand these pressures. Most of us are right here. We are progressing but we keep struggling against worry and wealth. The maybes and money issues sap our strength and put us at risk.

Like a trout's need for deep waters, we need roots that go down deep. Thus we gain stability. Drink in life-giving water and minerals. Stay healthy and grow strong.

So who is the man enjoying the growth from good soil? Jesus said, "The seed that fell on good soil is the man who hears the word and understands it" (verse 23). Spending time in God's Word and seeking to comprehend what it means — and what it means in our lives, day by day — is Jesus' plan for developing our strong, deep, root systems.

The result of deep roots is productivity . . . and reproductivity. With deep roots we can do what we were intended to do all along. We can multiply our lives in others, striving to fill the kingdom-lake to capacity.

FISHING DEEPER
READ HEBREWS 5:11–6:3

- Are you mature enough to feed yourself solid food? How do you know?
- Are you ready to be a teacher of others? Why?

TWENTY-TWO

CATCH AND RELEASE

THE GENERATIONS OF FISHERMEN THAT PRECEDED US ENJOYED what appeared to be a limitless supply of fish. As a high school student in the 60s, I would hike with friends to lakes in the Cascade mountains and catch fish all day long. We ate all we could for breakfast, lunch, and dinner and then packed the rest in snow and carried them home on our backs. It never crossed our minds that the supply might not keep up with the demand. Surely this well had no bottom!

But there is, indeed, a limited supply. Over fishing created part of the problem, but environmental hazards have added significantly to reducing the fish population in many areas. And although cleaner water and more controlled fishing have helped restore the size and quantity of fish in many parts of the country, the problems still exist.

There has been progress, though. Many fishermen have done their part by following the policy of catch and release.

A Freeing Experience
Catch and release provides the challenge of outsmarting a fish, the thrill of the strike, and the technique of playing and landing the fish. After a brief photo op the fish swims off, vowing to be more thoughtful about tomorrow's lunch selection. If however,

the fish is a slow learner, he will provide excitement for another angler, another day.

An amazing aspect of Christianity is that God is, in a sense, a catch and release fisherman. We see this, for instance, when Jesus used the imagery of fishing to explain to Peter the role of bringing people to Himself. Fishing was the occupation of one-third of Jesus' disciples and I'm sure the others got a full dose of fish stories during their years together. They understood the fishers of men imagery and the need to draw nets of compassion, instruction, and inspiration around those whom they encountered. Catch and release, however, was a new concept to all of them.

Yet catching people, the way God does it, always involves release—in two forms. The first involves what we are released *from*; the second involves what we are released *to*. In Romans 8:1-2 we read, "Therefore, there is now no condemnation for those who are in Christ Jesus, because through Christ Jesus the law of the Spirit of life set me free."

When Christ catches us, He releases us from the penalty of our sin—an eternal death sentence ("The wages of sin is death," Romans 6:23). Jesus' death on the cross paid the price and released us from this fate, but it's important to understand that being released from the death penalty of sin doesn't merely reduce our punishment to a life sentence. We are truly free from sin and no longer live life under its power. Unfortunately, we aren't out of the *presence* of sin until we reach heaven. We may often choose to sin, but we have been released from sin's controlling power and dominance in our lives.

Not only are we released *from* sin's penalty and power, but we are released *to* a new life of righteousness. Romans 6:18 says, "You have been set free from sin and have become slaves to righteousness." We gave up condemnation; we gained righteousness.

When God caught and released us, He *took away* what we could not get rid of on our own. There was no other option for us to gain release from sin. We could be good, but not good enough to undo the sins of our past. We could do good deeds, but never enough to compensate for our sinfulness. We could give money to the work of the Lord, but all our wealth couldn't begin to pay the debt we owed.

When God caught and released us, He *gave us* what we could not acquire for ourselves. We could provide acts of service and be morally pure, but as the prophet said: "All our righteous acts are like filthy rags" (Isaiah 64:6). Our best efforts are always tainted by multiple motives and limited ability. Our personal righteousness is not enough, so God releases us to a life lived in His righteousness.

The next time you play a fish into your net, unhook and release him, and think about what Christ has done for you. He caught you by His magnificent grace, and He released you to a marvelous freedom.

FISHING DEEPER
READ ROMANS 6:11-14

- What areas of sin still need to be "dethroned" in your life?
- In what ways could you offer yourself to God as an instrument of righteousness?

TWENTY-THREE

THE LAST CAST

I WAS COLD, WET, TIRED, AND SUNBURNED. MY BRUISED RIGHT knee ached from a fall earlier in the afternoon, the sun was going down, and I was ready to call it a day. Six of us had made the trip from Texas to New Mexico's San Juan River, and four had the good sense to return to Abe's Motel while a good time was still a good time. But Eldon and I weren't about to let misery interrupt a few more casts. There were still fish in Texas Hole, and we were going to get our money's worth. (I have a similar compulsion at all-you-can-eat buffets.)

The trophy waters of the San Juan allow you to take one trout, twenty inches or longer, each day. Once you have your fish, you're through for the day. Earlier that morning, Eldon had landed a twenty-two-inch trout that would have looked very nice mounted on his wall. But he didn't want the trophy badly enough to stop fishing.

The last hint of sunlight was turning dark purple when I saw Eldon set his hook and begin to play a real fighter. I noticed the time on my watch and then went about the business of playing a fish of my own. My fish performed what we call an SDR (short distance release), and I was quite sure he was several inches short of the twenty-inch requirement.

Enough was enough. By now it was dark, and I couldn't see

well enough to tie on a new fly. I became a spectator while Eldon battled his fish.

Over and over the fish would come close then turn and run, but each time with less strength. Seventeen minutes later fatigue overcame the gallant rainbow. It was now dark, but we could read the tape measure and the trout was just over nineteen inches—too short to keep.

I was gathering my things along the bank when I realized Eldon wasn't with me. I turned toward the river, and there he was, wading back into the dark water of Texas Hole.

"One more try," he said.

On his first cast the indicator moved. How he saw it I'll never know. The hook was set, and seven minutes later he landed a beautiful twenty-two-incher.

A Two-Sided Coin

My intrigue with time keeping was unrelated to any curiosity concerning how long it takes to land a fish. I just wanted to get dry, warm, and fed!

But Eldon had fulfilled his desire and lived his dream. He had persevered to the end. (As far as I was concerned, he had persevered way *beyond* the end.) Perseverance is staying power, the ability to see a job through to completion. As a two-sided coin, it involves active endurance and passive patience. In Colossians, Paul prays a wonderful prayer for these things:

And we pray this in order that you may live a life worthy of the Lord and may please him in every way: bearing fruit in every good work, growing in the knowledge of

God, being strengthened with all power according to his glorious might so that you may have great endurance and patience. (Colossians 1:10-11)

When I think of God's power, I usually think of the big challenges and projects of life. Surely I can handle the small stuff on my own; I only need God's help for the heroic tasks. Yet Paul prays for God's power so that perseverance will be a part of the Colossians' daily lives. He mentions both active endurance (which says, "I will keep going") and passive patience (which says, "I will wait faithfully").

The Colossian believers were facing theological heresy. But it could have been any challenge that required them to get up every morning and do the routine things that God expects.

Endurance is the antidote for the desire to quit doing what we know is right. It may be at work, at home, at church, or in the community. You may be overwhelmed with the routine of caring for a sick family member. You may be tired of your job. You may have taught the fifth-grade boys' Sunday school class for a long time. God's power is there to provide the endurance you need.

Then there's patience. It counteracts the desire to have our way right now—as we wait for God's timing. A child may be in rebellion, and we want things to change now. A business deal hinges on a decision that may never be made.

If you are like me, you want Christian maturity.

And you want it now.

God's power comes wrapped in the call to endurance and patience. The trophies come to us when we rely on God's power to strengthen us. And in His strength we learn to persevere for one more cast. To wait in the darkness one minute longer. To do the little things that matter most.

To wait patiently, yes . . . a little longer.

Just a little longer. . . .

FISHING DEEPER
READ GALATIANS 5:22-25

- How do the fruit of the Spirit relate to our need for perseverance?
- How would you rate yourself in the areas of patience and self-control?

TWENTY-FOUR

STAND AWAY, BOYS!

DEPENDING ON YOUR POINT OF VIEW, THE BOAT WAS EITHER "handcrafted" . . . or homemade. It came from my uncle's garage and contained enough wood to build a small city. The trailer was also an original, with car tires, carpeted skids, and a hand winch that would slowly but surely pull the boat out of the water and onto the trailer.

My two brothers and I were still school age when we set out one day with that row boat. Dad and Grandpa were taking us for an afternoon excursion of catfishing on Sturgeon Lake — a muddy, backwater lagoon outside of Portland on Sauvie Island. And the five Bolin men made quite a crew.

Every time we launched the boat on one of these trips, Grandpa told us about the time I fell off the dock into the Willamette Slough. This was always a delight to my brothers. The story was retold often enough that Grandpa, who loved poetry, reduced it to verse. I have the handwritten version in a frame in my bedroom and the final verse goes like this:

We pulled into the dockside;
Dan did not stop to think.
He reached too far to starboard
and landed in the drink.

Anyway, on this particular trip, we fished during the afternoon and then returned to the rocky beach we'd used as a makeshift boat ramp. Dad backed the trailer to the water's edge, but the surface and embankment made it difficult to back it too far into the lake.

Jim and I then manned the winch. The arm moved slowly, but we were making steady progress. Paul helped Dad push from the stern, and Grandpa was given some busywork to keep him from hurting himself.

But then Grandpa decided to take over. . . .

Good Work — Interrupted

"Stand away, boys!" Grandpa hollered.

What else could we do? Yes, Grandpa was old, his legs were chalky white, but he was a tough Swede who'd worked the lumber business most of his eighty years. We stepped back and let him have the winch handle. And with one mighty burst of power, he thrust it into motion.

For every force there is an equal and opposite reaction, or something like that. Well, it's true. The cable snapped as it was ripped from the bow of the boat. There we were, the boat half way off the trailer, the only means of moving it torn to bits. There is some other saying about good intentions . . . .

I really don't remember how we got the boat on the trailer, but we did. And the infamous phrase is now a family treasure. Even now, in our midforties, we brothers can still make each other laugh with a well-timed, "Stand away, boys!"

Those of us who are graying at the temples have a tendency to think and act like Grandpa. It's easy for us to disregard the efforts of youth. In the Bible, Timothy was a sensitive and insecure young man who, as a fledgling pastor, was in way over his head. But Paul writes to him and encourages him with these words:

Don't let anyone look down on you because you are young, but set an example for the believers in speech, in life, in love, in faith, and in purity. (1 Timothy 4:12)

If you are young, the directive is obvious: Don't let your youth keep you from making an impact with your life. Don't use your age as an excuse for failure or inactivity. And certainly don't forget that you can be an example to the rest of us.

If, on the other hand, you have walked a little farther down life's road, don't assume that your ways are always superior or that the methods of the next generation are always suspect. Provide opportunities and encouragement for young people.

And whatever you do, don't interrupt a good work by telling everyone else to "Stand away, boys."

FISHING DEEPER
READ 1 KINGS 3:4-13

- How often is the word "servant" used in this passage?
- What relationship do you see between wisdom and servant-hood in your life?

TWENTY-FIVE

STRIKING SILVER

WHY WOULD A FISH BITE INTO A COLD, STEELY HOOK WITHOUT a morsel of food on it?

No bait, just a shiny silver hook.

When the herring were biting in Lincoln City—a wonderful little town perched along Highway 101 on the Oregon coast—fishermen and spectators would line Taft Dock as buckets of the little silver fish were hauled over the railings. The equipment was clean and simple. At the end of the line dangled a half-ounce weight with five silver hooks preceding it in six-inch intervals.

No fish food. Hooks.

For hours folks would cast and retrieve the line with a jerking motion, giving the weight and hooks the appearance of silver, minnow-like fish. The herring must have assumed the flashing silver hooks were creatures below them on the food chain. They struck at the silver flash and became dead meat. When I tried it, I'd catch two or three with each cast. The action was fast, furious, and fun.

Seeing the Big Picture

What's wrong with herrings' eyes? All of us on the dock could see that the hooks were hooks. We all knew there was no bait disguising the cold, silver steel. Were their eyes playing tricks on them?

Certainly our spiritual eyes play tricks on us. They have a tendency to focus on problems, failing to see God's strength and provision.

Take the case of Elisha's servant. Elisha was one of the great prophets during the time of Israel's kings. At one point in Elisha's life and ministry, the king of Aram waged war with Israel. But each time the king maneuvered his army to ambush the Israelite army, Elisha would receive a message from God revealing the trap.

This happened so often that the king of Aram assumed Elisha had a spy in his inner circle. He was enraged and demanded an explanation. One of his officers gave him this report, "Elisha, the prophet who is in Israel, tells the king of Israel the very words you speak in your bedroom" (2 Kings 6:12).

The solution seemed simple enough: capture Elisha and cut off the flow of information. At the time, Elisha was living in the small town of Dothan. So one night a large army with horses and chariots surrounded the city. Early in the morning Elisha's servant was up performing his duties and saw the army encircling the city. He rushed to Elisha in a panic,

"O, my lord, what shall we do?" the servant asked. "Don't be afraid," the prophet answered. "Those who are with us are more than those that are with them." And Elisha prayed, "O Lord, open his eyes so he may see." Then the Lord opened the servant's eyes, and he looked and saw the

hills full of horses and chariots of fire all around Elisha.
(2 Kings 6:15-17)

Elisha's spiritual eyesight was extraordinary. His servant's vision was more like a herring's—and ours. Isn't our spiritual vision often shortsighted? And we seem to have an ongoing problem with focus.

The servant could see just far enough to comprehend the danger and the huge problem facing Dothan. But he couldn't see well enough to realize God's power and protection just beyond his sight. When we lose sight of the big picture, we can only focus on the parts. Fear and panic result.

What danger are you facing today? Have you tried stepping back for a moment to let the full picture come into view?

Looking Beyond the Short Term

Elisha looked out at the hills and saw chariots of fire. But he also saw beyond the issues of warfare, with its short-term victories and defeats. He apparently understood the need for ultimate resolution of the conflict and the need to establish friendly relationships.

The prophet prayed that Aram's soldiers would be blinded. Seeing their vulnerable condition, the king of Israel asked if he should kill them. He focused on immediate victory rather than preparing for the long-term relationship.

Elisha's response was to restore their sight, fix a great feast, then send them home. The army of Aram was now populated with grateful soldiers who owed their lives to the Israelites. "So the bands from Aram stopped raiding Israel's territory" (2 Kings 6:23).

Of course, that's what Israel had wanted all along. And the ability to see the big picture—the things that are truly important in the long run—made it all happen.

FISHING DEEPER
READ 1 PETER 1:3-9

- How difficult is it for you to love and believe in someone you have never seen?
- How does your understanding of the unseen affect your attitude toward your problems?

TWENTY-SIX

SCHOOL'S OUT

I LOVE WATCHING FISH MOVE IN SCHOOLS. THE SHIMMERING onslaught of color, the reckless, slapdash careening. The whole gyrating throng racing by in a blur of flashing fins.

What marvelous choreography!

The entire group acts as a single unit, moving together in one direction and then pivoting as one to dash away. Each fish has its own mind, but each chooses to follow the group.

Yet where are they going? Who's giving direction?

No doubt there is some purpose here. I've heard that schooling makes the small fish look bigger and more imposing to large predators. Others have said that schooling motions confuse predators that would love to just relax and feast more leisurely.

At any rate, I'm sure God designed fish to swim in schools for a reason. It's so beautiful, and so functional.

Going Along?

Going along with the group may protect small fish, but following the crowd can put people in danger. In our world the majority is frequently wrong; God often siding with the minority. It's important, then, to regularly ponder: *Am I moving in a "school" that's moving away from God?*

Psalm 1 addresses the issue of the crowd's influence in our lives, highlighting two pressures that determine our choices and shape our characters: the desire to please our friends and the call to obey God's Word. Sometimes we can do both; usually we must choose only one.

> *How blessed is the man who does not walk in the counsel of*
> *the wicked,*
> *Nor stand in the path of sinners,*
> *Nor sit in the seat of scoffers!*
> *But his delight is in the law of the LORD,*
> *And in His law he meditates day and night.* (verses 1-2)

The poem opens by describing what a godly man avoids. He rejects the temptation to join the school. He doesn't get involved in the downward spiral of walking near, standing by, or participating in sinful activities. The direction for his life doesn't come from peer pressures around him; rather, he delights in God's Word day and night.

I hate to admit it, but when facing tough decisions, my first thought is often: "What will *they* think?" (Insert your own unique "they.") Can you relate?

But suppose we immediately asked ourselves: "What will God think?" I know that by spending time reading, studying, and thinking about God's Word our minds can begin moving in tandem with the mind of God instead of moving in sync with the crowd.

The third and fourth verses of this little psalm paint pictures of two lives. The first is influenced by God's Word, the second by the pressures of the "school."

And he will be like a tree firmly planted by streams of water,
Which yields its fruit in its season,
And its leaf does not wither;
And in whatever he does, he prospers.

The tree pictures a man who provides comfort and strength to those who come to him. His leaves provide shade, his fruits provide nourishment, and his very presence gives direction to wanderers seeking guidance. Even though he lives in the heat of the scorching sun and is battered by the storms of life, he remains firm and fruitful. When the winds blow, his branches bend, his leaves flutter, but his trunk stays unmoved, his roots firm.

This stability and strength comes to the person who clings day and night to God's Word. But the next verse is one of the most pathetic in all of Scripture.

The wicked are not so,
They are like the chaff which the wind drives away.

The same winds that drive the chaff, rustle the leaves of the tree. The tree takes the hit and recovers. The chaff flies away. It's a description of the lifeless husks that protect developing heads of grain. At harvest time they are crushed and driven away by the breeze. We've all seen it: the winds of outside influence dictate the course of a wasted, futile, lifeless existence.

Or Individual Choices?

Notice that the first three verses speak of an individual, but verse four changes to the plural. I hear the psalmist saying that a righteous life won't blossom by committee or spring up as a crowd. Swimming with the school is too mindless, too convenient, to allow for the rigorous disciplines of spiritual growth. Rather, it has to do with the very personal, rational choices each of us makes, day by day. It has to do with continually asking: *What's influencing my thinking at the moment? What delights my heart today? Where am I getting my direction for tomorrow? Am I moving with the temptations of the world, the changing directions of its cultural currents?*

Schools of fish dart one way, then another. And we, too, will flit around aimlessly if our guidance comes from the swimmers around us.

Yes, schooling provides safety for fish. But it can be quite dangerous for the rest of us.

FISHING DEEPER
READ LUKE 17:11-19

- When have you found yourself "going with the crowd" while knowing you were traveling in the wrong direction? What were the consequences?
- What does this reveal about your perspective on God's power and authority in your life?

TWENTY-SEVEN

FEEDING TIME

THE RUBBER RAFT LOST SOME PRESSURE WHEN I MOVED IT OUT of the warm sunshine into the ice-cold waters of Trillium Lake. The manufacturer said the little yellow boat was designed for two people, but I filled most of it myself. The strap seat sagged as my weight came down on it, and the water under the canvas bottom bulged up, creating an odd-looking mound below my feet. Two short aluminum oars and a gusty wind made maneuvering quite difficult.

To make things even more comfortable, the water dripping from the oars began accumulating beneath me. And since my weight created a depression in the canvas hull, soon my bottom and legs were soaking wet with what had recently been a snow field on Mount Hood.

Of course, nothing was biting. The only thing worse than the condition of the boat was the apparent lack of fish until a tremendous opportunity plunked itself down right in front of me. . . .

A Great Opportunity
A gust of wind turned my beloved yacht toward the shore, and I noticed an unusual looking truck backing down the boat ramp. It was a tanker with a green emblem on the cab door. I drifted in the wind as I watched the driver attach a long black

hose to the tank, stretch it to the water, and turn a valve.

A dream come true! He was stocking the lake with thousands of ten-inch trout. I forgot my cold, wet condition and rowed for the fish. They were schooling along the top of the water, thrashing about, boiling the surface. I cast my lure into the turbulent mass. With thousands of fish in the area, the odds were definitely in my favor.

Nothing happened.

I cast time and time again. Nothing.

At least I wasn't alone. Others joined the frantic attempt to catch one of these new arrivals, but nothing worked. The fish were out of their comfortable environment, traumatized by their ride, and terrified by their new surroundings.

Those poor fish were paralyzed by the events in their lives. Their trauma had left them unable to feed themselves or behave in a reasonable manner. They were dominated by the fear.

A Terrible Robbery

Jehoshaphat certainly knew about fear. This ancient king faced a vast army, and the prospects of victory looked dim. But God sent a message saying, "Do not be afraid or discouraged because of this vast army, for the battle is not yours but God's" (2 Chronicles 20:15).

Would that kind of message help you? How would you respond? The temptation, when faced with tough transitions and difficult changes in our lives, is to stop our "spiritual feeding." A myriad of crises can induce spiritual anorexia. The only cure is to come back to the heavenly feast and indulge ourselves. Jesus reminded His disciples of their supply:

"I am the bread of life. Your forefathers ate the manna in the desert, yet they died. But here is the bread that comes down from heaven which a man may eat and not die. I am the living bread that came down from heaven."
(John 6:48-51)

There are really only two choices before us when the difficulties of life crash in upon us. One is to allow fear and anxiety to dominate, become overwhelmed by the trauma, and lose our appetite for the things of God. The other choice is to come to Christ and dine on the spiritual feast of His Word.

When have you been so disoriented, perplexed, or confused—that you forgot where the kitchen was? At those times we worry instead of trust, trade courage for cowardice, and react foolishly instead of responding thoughtfully.

Then our fear becomes a cruel thief. It robs us of peace, energy, and wisdom. Worst of all, it makes us act like trout fresh from a fish hatchery. We stop eating.

FISHING DEEPER
READ PSALM 119:65-72

- According to verse 71, what benefit is there to being in difficult situations?
- What is your typical reaction to difficult circumstances? Do you go first to God's Word, or do you find most of your support and comfort elsewhere?

TWENTY-EIGHT

A COMFORTABLE FIT

I THOUGHT THE PILE OF LEAVES HAD BURNED ITSELF OUT. I HAD raked and burned on Saturday, and then the following Tuesday I traveled out of town for an all-day meeting. When I returned home that evening, my wife composed herself and explained what had happened with that "burned out" leaf pile. . . .

Disaster!

Apparently some pretty strong midday winds had ignited a few still-smoldering leaves and blown some past the cleared ring of dirt into the brush nearby. The wind drove the fire toward our wooden storage building, which contained some of my most prized—as well as least loved—possessions.

I was left with one less storage shed and a handsome insurance check. Lawn mowers, leaf blowers, rakes, and shovels were long gone (and I didn't miss them a bit). My fishing rods and equipment were another story, however. I was compelled to replace them immediately.

In a matter of weeks everything was new: waders without patches, a vest with more pockets, a gleaming graphite rod.

New hat. New net.

But, of course, the clothes and equipment felt stiff and uncomfortable. Worst of all was the way they made me look. Like I was taking up fishing for the first time in my life.

115

A Whole New Outfit

When we become Christians we receive a whole new set of clothes and equipment to put on. Have you ever thought of it that way? This new outfit may feel uncomfortable, and we may sense that we are out of place in it. But the whole wardrobe is immensely better than what we were wearing before.

Colossians 3:12 and 14 tell of five new pieces of heavenly clothing, along with an overcoat that should cover all the rest:

> *Therefore, as God's chosen people, holy and dearly loved, clothe yourselves with compassion, kindness, humility, gentleness and patience. . . . And over all these virtues put on love, which binds them all together in perfect unity.*

Compassion is sensitivity to the hurts and needs of those around us. Unfortunately, it has become excess baggage in a world obsessed with gaining, accumulating, protecting, and achieving. How easy it is to let our hearts grow cold to the pain and problems around us!

But compassion needs shoes. To have a heart that is sensitive to the hurts of our world is a great starting point. But our empathy must blossom into action. *Kindness* is the behavior that flows from a heart of compassion. Through kindness we look for opportunities to lend a hand and lighten a load.

We could easily become prideful as we reflect on the compassion in our hearts and the kindness we're showing to those "less fortunate" around us. That's where *humility* comes in. By it we avoid comparisons, knowing that only by the grace of God does any creature live and breathe on this earth.

Gentleness comes next. We tend to equate gentleness with

weakness, but it is better understood as "strength under control." As we help others, and our attitude is right before God, we can develop the inner strength and control to use our energy and resources wisely.

Finally, can we make time for *patience?* The futurists of the previous generation worried about how we would spend our "extra" time as labor-saving devices became more and more commonplace. Today we are dealing with activity overload — and we need everything yesterday.

Yet we must put on patience. Why? Because things may not improve, even when our compassionate heart reaches out and does good deeds with the right motives and a gentle spirit. That is when we need patience. For God always works in his own time. It must become our time, too.

Binding together all of these great and godly virtues is *love.* It is our desire to provide the best for the object of our affection, and it requires taking an active part in the lives of those whom God brings into our world. If the other five virtues are in place and functioning, the natural result is love.

Suppose this new outfit doesn't feel comfortable at first? I suggest breaking it in through regular use. It will serve you well. Better than anything you've waded around in before.

FISHING DEEPER
READ JOB 29:14-17

- How did putting on righteousness and justice impact Job?
- What one character trait would you like to put on — and become comfortable wearing?

SOCIAL SECURITY BEACH

As a teenager, one of my favorite pastimes was going to Sauvie Island during salmon runs. My father and I would cast our Spin-N-Glow lures as far into the Columbia River as possible, plant our poles in the sand, attach a bell to their tips, and retreat back up the bank. There we'd sit on a piece of driftwood or stand around a warm fire.

And wait. Expectantly.

Hundreds of senior citizens always lined the sandy bank of the river, giving it the name Social Security Beach. Most of these folks had fished the salmon runs for decades. Each fisherman had experienced the exhilaration of hearing his bell clang as a silver or chinook hit his lure. They had all raced to their pole and fought a gallant fish onto the beach. And all had experienced the frustration of the line going slack.

Bested by an animal with a brain the size of an acorn!

It Becomes Second Nature

These fishermen were ending their lives the way they had lived them. They'd developed patterns for their days and for the seasons of the year. The choices they made, day in and day out, had become second nature. "The salmon are running; it's time to go fishing," they would say as they put their gear in the car and headed for their favorite waters. They had made this choice so often it was barely considered a choice at all.

Have you noticed that the choices we make every day are establishing the lifestyles we'll have at the end of our lives? I think of the apostle Paul writing to Timothy. It was toward the end of Paul's life, and he looked back over the choices he had made across the decades. He said, "I have fought a good fight, I have finished the race, I have kept the faith. Now there is in store for me the crown of righteousness" (2 Timothy 4:7-8).

The key to Paul ending well was the little choices he had made all along the way. First, Paul had chosen to "fight the good fight." God didn't remove His servant from the difficult situations he faced, and Paul knew that life was a fight—a good fight—but a fight nonetheless.

You may be fighting the good fight today with cancer, with an unreasonable boss, with a child who is making destructive choices, or with a mate who is unfaithful. God calls you to keep fighting the good fight. *To end* strong we must stay in the ring until the final bell sounds.

Second, Paul chose to "finish the course." The old fishermen weren't going to let the salmon run pass them by. They had set their pattern of participation early in life and each opportunity had become a fresh challenge. Today you and I will have opportunities to share our faith, encourage a brother, or help someone in need. If we want to finish strong we'll need to establish godly patterns of service and obedience along the way.

Fighting and finishing are of eternal value only when we accomplish them in the context of a third requirement for ending well: ongoing trust—that is, "keeping the faith." Have you ever meditated upon the achievements of the spiritual giants listed in Hebrews 11, the Faith Hall of Fame? Notice that they are always preceded with the words, "by faith." How did Noah, Abraham, Moses, Gideon, David, Jeremiah, and the others fight and finish? The same way we are to fight and finish today: by faith.

Yes, any of us can choose to fight the good fight, finish the course, and keep the faith. I'm inspired to do it, especially when I remember that the only way to end well is to live well along the way.

FISHING DEEPER
READ JOSHUA 1:6-9; 23:1-10

- What themes were important to Joshua at the beginning and the end of his life?
- What could you do today to help develop the themes that you want to dominate the conclusion of your life?

THIRTY

A STEP AHEAD

THE OLDER I GET THE MORE I APPRECIATE FISHING WITH A guide. In my younger days I wouldn't think of stooping to such depths. I felt confident in my knowledge and abilities, certain that my own "fish smarts" could match any professional's.

I've changed my mind. Perhaps I've become more realistic about my ability—or inability. Maybe I have less time to invest in fishing and want to maximize my efforts. The cost of getting from Texas to trout country is substantial, and in some ways a guide is like buying insurance on the overall cost of the trip.

In reality, I probably want someone to blame if I come home empty-handed. But a guide is definitely worth his wages when I'm catching fish. He knows the area. And he's already aware of the submerged logs and hidden coves where the fish congregate.

Guides also provide instruction. I have much better technique, distance, and accuracy with a fly rod because guides have taught me. I learned several new knots and am aware of the latest fishing gadgets because I've listened to guides. They're professionals, and if I'm willing to learn I come away with a net full of useful information.

A good guide can spoil you, too. He untangles knots, rows the boat, and fixes lunch. His job is to care for the detail work, so I can keep fishing.

Have One . . . and Be One

In the spiritual realm, God wants us to *have* guides so we can build on the wisdom of those who have gone before us. But God also wants us to *be* guides, to help those who are following in our footsteps.

Young John Mark needed a guide. His family was active in Jerusalem's early church, and the first prayer meetings gathered in his parents' home. He accompanied his cousin Barnabas and the apostle Paul on the first missionary journey. But not too long into the trip John Mark turned back, and we don't know exactly why. Was he just homesick? Or frightened? Had he become jealous as Paul seemed to bypass his cousin Barnabas? Or was it a theological disagreement? Whatever the reason, John Mark cut his journey short and abandoned his commitment.

Yet when the time came for a second missionary trip, John Mark again volunteered. Acts 15:36-39 tells what happened:

> *Some time later Paul said to Barnabas, "Let us go back and visit the brothers in all the towns where we preached the word of the Lord and see how they are doing." Barnabas wanted to take John, also called Mark, with them, but Paul did not think it wise to take him because he had deserted them in Pamphylia and had not continued with them in the work. They had such a sharp disagreement that they parted company. Barnabas took Mark and sailed for Cyprus but Paul chose Silas.*

Barnabas became a guide and John Mark became a willing follower. Over their years of ministry together, Barnabas was able to help this young man immensely. He certainly helped

John Mark stay out of more trouble, as the boy learned the dangers and pitfalls of bad decisions. And John Mark learned how to spot opportunities for service.

John Mark had needed someone to untangle the messes in his life and help steer him in the right direction. Apparently it worked well: he went on to pen the Gospel of Mark. And near the end of his life, Paul wrote to his friend Timothy and said, "Get Mark and bring him with you, because he is helpful to me in my ministry" (2 Timothy 4:11).

Nice round trip for a guy who just needed a little guidance.

Of course, each of us needs our Barnabas, the man of experience who gives us direction, encouragement, and councel. But we also need a John Mark in our lives, someone to nurture along in godly wisdom. Our own children, young people in our church or in the community, all are desperate for a caring individual to point them in the right direction. Barnabas went the extra mile to do it. You can too.

FISHING DEEPER
READ PROVERBS 3:1-12

- What are the benefits of having a mentor and being a mentor?
- What will you need to change in order to become a better guide to those who may follow in your footsteps?

THIRTY ONE

THOUGHTS FROM THE THICKET

THROUGH THE AGE OF TWELVE, I WAS GRANTED COMPLIMEN-
tary fishing rights in Oregon. But once I turned thirteen, the
free ride was over.

So here was my thinking at the time: *Okay, now I'm thirteen.
But summer's almost over! Am I really going to spend my hard-
earned berry picking money on a fishing license? A permit that's
going to expire in a few short weeks? I don't think so. . . .*

Run and Hide!
My friend Pat and I were serious fishermen who would wet a
line every chance we could. One sunny August day, a few weeks
after my birthday, Pat's mom dropped us off along with my
younger brother, Paul, at a backwater lagoon near the conver-
gence of the Willamette and Columbia rivers.

We fished below a railroad bridge supported by a tall con-
crete wall. A few feet above the water level the wall widened to
provide a walkway where we could sit and fish. About a dozen
people were there trying to bring home a catfish for dinner.
Mainly they were just reducing the carp population.

The sunny day of fishing bliss was interrupted by a small
commotion to my left. My blood ran cold when I saw a light
brown shirt with the dark green arm patches moving toward me.

Game warden!

He was still at the far end of the walkway, checking licenses and slowly moving my way. Pat had a license and my brother was only eleven, but I knew I was in big trouble if I didn't do something quickly. While the warden checked a man at the far end of the wall, I left my pole, slipped around the corner, ran up an embankment over the highway, and hid in a blackberry thicket. From my hiding place I could see under the highway bridge to the railroad bridge support where Pat and Paul kept fishing. Through the vines I spotted the warden. I watched him for a few minutes, and then he was out of view.

I waited a long, long time. Never sure if he was creeping toward my hiding place, lurking behind a tree, waiting to nab me when I showed myself. Or had he gone on to solve even bigger crimes? Eventually, I assumed the coast was clear, came out of hiding, and returned to my fishing.

Next year I bought a license.

It's the First Thing We Do

When we are in the wrong, and we know it, our first instinct is to run and hide. I did it with the game warden, and Adam and Eve did it with God in the Garden. After the first sin, Adam and Eve realized their shame and knew that something had gone wrong. We pick up the story in Genesis 3:7-10:

> *Then the eyes of both of them were opened, and they realized they were naked; so they sewed fig leaves together and made coverings for themselves. Then the man and his wife heard the sound of the Lord God as he was walking in*

125

the garden in the cool of the day, and they hid from the
Lord God among the trees of the garden. But the Lord God
called to the man, "Where are you?" He answered, "I
heard you in the garden, and I was afraid."

Fear drives us into hiding and away from the place of restoration and salvation. Shame and guilt separate us from the one who can restore the fellowship we so desperately miss. We come to our senses in a berry thicket, hoping God didn't notice our rebellion, certain that if He found out He would come after us with a big stick.

We forget that the punishment has already been exacted. In His love for us, God sent His son to be our substitute and to take the death sentence that had been pronounced upon us as sinners. Our sin is serious, but God's love is greater.

He still comes to the garden in the cool of the day to call for us. He offers a relationship based on His love for us, not upon any goodness and purity in our lives. He wants us to live holy lives, but for our benefit as much as His.

If you have never put your trust in Jesus, today would be a great day to do it. Crawl back out of the berry thicket where you've been hiding. Accept the fact that you have fallen short of God's perfection—and accept your "permit" into eternal life.

FISHING DEEPER
READ JONAH 1:1-15

- In what ways could you say you are "running from God"?
- Who else might be in danger because of your flight?

ABOUT THE AUTHOR

DAN BOLIN IS THE PRESIDENT OF DAN BOLIN RESOURCE, INC., WHICH provides ministry, marketing, management, and fundraising support to Christian nonprofit ministries. He is also a senior associate with the Goehner Resource Group and a regional representative for Christian Camping International.

Dan earned his bachelor's degree from Seattle Pacific University and his master's of theology degree from Dallas Theological Seminary. He also holds an MBA from LeTourneu University.

A frequent speaker both nationally and internationally, Dan is the author or coauthor of several books, including *The One That Got Away, Avoiding the Blitz, How to Be Your Daughter's Daddy, How to Be Your Little Man's Dad,* and *How to Be Your Wife's Best Friend.* He has also been published in *Decision Magazine* and *The Journal of Christian Camping.*

Dan, his wife Cay, and their daughter Haley live near Tyler, Texas, where he serves as an elder at Bethel Bible Church and as a board member of Dan Anderson Ministries and the Tyler Independent School District.

If you liked THE ONE THAT GOT AWAY, be sure to check out these other men's books from NavPress!

Avoiding the Blitz

This fun devotional based on football is the perfect gift for avid football fans. Each short devotional highlights an element of football, applying a spiritual truth and lesson for life. Great for gift giving!

Avoiding the Blitz
(Dan Bolin) $10

Becoming a Man of Prayer

Based on Jesus' instructions, this book will help you pray consistently—starting with five minutes each day to an hour spent in prayer. Includes discussion questions.

Becoming a Man of Prayer
(Bob Beltz) $10

Dangers Men Face

Being prepared can make all the difference when it comes to danger. Learn five common dangers that men face in life and be prepared to deal with these dangers head-on. Includes discussion questions.

Dangers Men Face
(Jerry White) $14

Get your copies today at your local bookstore, or call (800) 366-7788 and ask for offer **#2132**.

NAVPRESS
BRINGING TRUTH TO LIFE
www.navpress.com

Prices subject to change without notice.